ORANGES AND LEMONS

RHYMES FROM PAST TIMES

For my mother,
Hazel Cooper

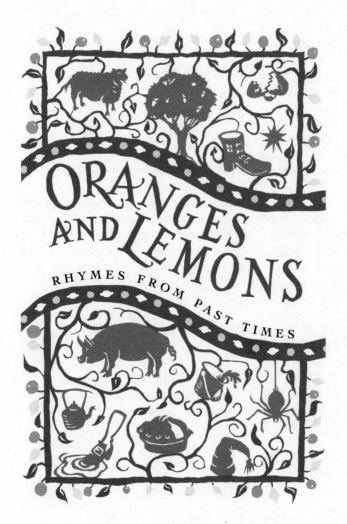

ORANGES AND LEMONS

RHYMES FROM PAST TIMES

KAREN DOLBY

Michael O'Mara Books Limited

This paperback edition first published in 2015

First published in Great Britain in 2012 by
Michael O'Mara Books Limited
9 Lion Yard
Tremadoc Road
London SW4 7NQ

A CIP catalogue record for this book is available from the British Library.

Papers used by Michael O'Mara Books Limited are natural, recyclable products made from wood grown in sustainable forests. The manufacturing processes conform to the environmental regulations of the country of origin.

ISBN: 978-1-78243-485-6 in paperback print format
ISBN: 978-1-84317-975-7 in EPub format
ISBN: 978-1-84317-976-4 in Mobipocket format

1 2 3 4 5 6 7 8 9 10

Cover illustration and design by Patrick Knowles
Designed and typeset by K DESIGN, Winscombe, Somerset
Printed and bound by CPI Group (UK) Ltd, Croydon, CR0 4YY

www.mombooks.com

Contents

Monday's Child: The Rhythm of Days **45**

Humpty Dumpty: Royal Connections **51**

Oranges and Lemons: Songs and Games 119

Do You Know the Muffin Man?: Street Cries and Action Rhymes

It's Raining, It's Pouring: Weather Wise and Warnings

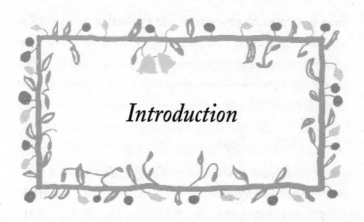

Introduction

When I came to write this book, I was surprised how clearly I could remember the words to many of the nursery rhymes I learned as a young child. The verses are apparently effortlessly fixed in my memory when it seems so easy to forget much of what I've carefully tried to learn since.

For many of us, nursery rhymes are the first verses we hear, the first lines we learn by heart. They are interwoven with our earliest memories, whether miming the actions, learning to count, or simply enjoying the rhythm and sound of the words and lines. I can still remember the book of rhymes I looked at with my mother when I was very small, and picture the illustrations. I think this is true for many people and probably the reason why nursery rhymes are so fondly remembered and firmly lodged in our consciousness.

The majority of the rhymes are anonymous, part of an oral tradition of folk memories passed on by word of mouth from generation to generation. They were first written down on broadsheets and in chapbooks, often little more than pamphlets, containing poems, stories, songs and religious tracts, illustrated with engravings which made them popular with the many people at the time who were unable to read.

In most cases, nursery rhymes were only collected into published books from the eighteenth century onwards when a growing interest in children's literature developed. The first anthology was *Tommy Thumb's Pretty Song Book*, which was printed in London around 1744. Others quickly followed. Specific melodies or games were also often associated with the rhymes and these were very widely known.

But nursery rhymes are so much more than simple verses for children. Some have a decidedly sinister edge, which is perhaps why they have been used to such chilling effect in horror films. Many are very old, dating back to the Elizabethan era, and some even further to medieval ballads, or classical odes. They may recall past events and characters otherwise long forgotten, or parody royalty and political figures from a time when open dissent was a serious offence.

Some of the oldest rhymes have the best-documented histories, for others the origins are completely hidden, and although there are theories, it is impossible to know for certain what is true and what is just a good tale. Over the centuries, the distinction between myth and history can become blurred. Perhaps that's part of their charm, and decoding the hidden meanings offers a tantalizing glimpse of the past and a fascinating insight into our social history.

The most innocent-sounding little rhymes can hide the most surprising stories: for instance, was little Jack Horner a sixteenth-century chancer who took advantage of a trusting boss and turbulent times to advance his family fortunes? And folklore suggests the rhyming couplet, 'When Adam delved and Eve span, Who was then a gentleman?' dates from the years following the Black Death. Referring to the equality known in the Garden of Eden, it was used as a rally call to revolution, a cry for freedom from the rigid feudal system, which helped to fire the movement leading to the Peasants' Revolt in 1381. However, although it's a popular idea, 'Ring-A-Ring O' Roses' is probably not linked to the Great Plague. It may not even be particularly old, not appearing in the earliest anthologies.

There are references to nursery rhymes in Shakespeare and Pepys, in eighteenth-century pantomimes and early scientific studies. There are remarkable similarities between the rhymes told in Britain, America and throughout Europe.

'Humpty Dumpty' becomes '*Humpelken-Pumpelken*' in Germany, and '*Boule, boule*' in France.

Oranges And Lemons is a collection of the most well-known and best-loved nursery rhymes, along with some that may be less familiar. The book looks at the history of the rhymes and the controversies surrounding their origins. Although children throughout the ages demand that rhymes be told 'again' in exactly the same way, variations in wording have evolved. The versions I have included are the ones I remember, the rhymes I have tried to pass on to my own children, and I apologize if they differ from the versions you knew and loved.

Acknowledgements

Thanks to everyone who passed on their favourite rhymes and stories, and to the editorial and design teams at Michael O'Mara, especially Louise Dixon and Patrick Knowles.

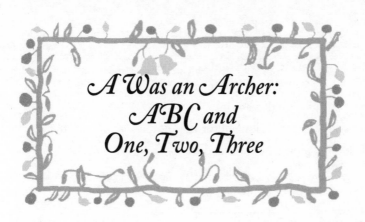

A Was an Archer: ABC and One, Two, Three

Alphabet rhymes have always been popular as a fun way to help children learn to read, and their vivid imagery lends itself to lively illustrations. Counting-out rhymes are remarkably international and many are variations of the same ancient codes. Used as a formula for choosing who is 'it' in children's games, their apparent simplicity may hide a more sinister past.

A Was an Apple Pie

A was an apple pie;
B bit it,
C cut it,
D dealt it,
E eat it,
F fought for it,

G got it,
H had it,
I inspected it,
J jumped for it,
K kept it,
L longed for it,
M mourned for it,
N nodded at it,
O opened it,
P peeped in it,
Q quartered it,
R ran for it,
S stole it,
T took it,
U upset it,
V viewed it,
W wanted it,
X, Y, Z, and ampersand
All wished for a piece in hand.

This simple rhyme, teaching the alphabet, has a long history and was known in the reign of Charles II, when letters A to G were quoted in a religious pamphlet. The vowels I and U are also missing from other early versions as no distinction used to be made between the letters I and J, and U and V when written as capitals.

It was published in a children's spelling book in 1742 in London, and first printed in America in 1750 in Boston.

After that, it often appeared in eighteenth-century chapbooks and by the beginning of the nineteenth century there were many variations. Kate Greenaway's illustrated edition has remained in print since its first appearance in 1886 and is one of the best known, but there are also parodies by writers such as Edward Lear.

A Was an Archer

A was an archer, who shot at a frog,
B was a butcher, and had a great dog.
C was a captain, all covered with lace,
D was a drunkard, and had a red face.
E was an esquire, with pride on his brow,
F was a farmer, and followed the plow.
G was a gamester, who had but ill luck,
H was a hunter, and hunted a buck.
I was an innkeeper, who loved to carouse,
J was a joiner, and built up a house.
K was King William, once governed this land,
L was a lady, who had a white hand.
M was a miser, and hoarded up gold,
N was a nobleman, gallant and bold.
O was an oyster girl, and went about town,
P was a parson, and wore a black gown.
Q was a queen, who wore a silk slip,
R was a robber, and wanted a whip.
S was a sailor, and spent all he got,

T was a tinker, and mended a pot.

U was an usurer, a miserable elf,

V was a vintner, who drank all himself.

W was a watchman, and guarded the door,

X was expensive, and so became poor.

Y was a youth, that did not love school,

Z was a zany, a poor harmless fool.

This is probably the best known of the ABC rhymes today and is often called 'Tom Thumb's Alphabet'. It is relatively recent in nursery-rhyme terms – little more than a hundred and fifty years old – but there is an older version dating from Queen Anne's reign where C is a cutpurse, K a knave, and Y a yeoman who worked for his bread.

New alphabet books are still being produced – one of the best twentieth-century versions is the mock alphabet by Edward Gorey. With a surreal humour, *The Gashlycrumb Tinies* outlines the grisly deaths of the twenty-six tinies: 'A is for Amy, who fell down the stairs, B is for Basil, assaulted by bears', and so on, each with a gothic black-and-white illustration.

Eeny, Meeny, Miny, Mo

Eeny, meeny, miny, mo,
Catch a tiger by his toe,
If he hollers let him go.
Eeny, meeny, miny, mo.

The middle two lines have been constantly adapted over the years in line with political correctness, but 'Eeny, meeny, miny, mo' harks back to ancient Celtic numbers and is surprisingly widespread, with echoes across Europe and in the US. This is one of the most well known of the counting-out rhymes used by children to decide who is 'it' in a game. There may be a rather macabre origin to the practice: one theory is that Druid priests chanted 'eena, meena, mina, mo' to decide which unlucky victim to sacrifice.

Counting-out rhymes also link with archaic shepherds' scores for counting sheep, for instance: 'Yan, tan, tethera, pethera, pimp' from Westmorland, and 'Een, teen, tether, fether, fip', which is known as Indian counting in America.

One For Sorrow

> One for sorrow, two for joy,
> Three for a girl, four for a boy,
> Five for silver, six for gold,
> Seven for a secret never to be told.
> Eight for a wish, nine for a kiss,
> Ten for a bird you must not miss.

The oldest recorded versions from the eighteenth century begin with, 'One for sorrow, two for mirth, three for a wedding, four for a birth'. The rhyme has always been associated with superstitions surrounding magpies, although it sometimes refers to other members of the crow family including ravens, rooks, jackdaws and jays.

Magpies and crows have been viewed with suspicion since ancient times and ravens were known as the 'devil's bird', feared as omens of bad luck and even death. Like many other birds, magpies and crows are as likely to appear alone as in pairs or varying-sized flocks, which is perhaps why the numbers seen together were thought to be so significant. Also, they are very showy birds, easy to spot and count.

One, Two, Buckle My Shoe

One, two,
Buckle my shoe;
Three, four,
Knock at the door;
Five, six,
Pick up sticks;
Seven, eight,
Lay them straight;
Nine, ten,
A big fat hen;
Eleven, twelve,
Dig and delve;
Thirteen, fourteen,
Maids a-courting;
Fifteen, sixteen,

Maids a-kissing;
Seventeen, eighteen,
Maids a-waiting;
Nineteen, twenty,
My plate's empty.

This popular counting rhyme was first published in 1805 in *Songs For The Nursery*, although it is thought to be much older. Henry Carrington Bolton, a Victorian collector of counting rhymes, recorded several different versions, one going up to thirty, and he believed the rhyme was 'used in Wrentham, Massachusetts, as early as 1780'. The lines 'pick up sticks' and 'lay them straight' have been linked to lacemaking but there seems to be no firm evidence for this. The same general form is also well known throughout France, Germany, Turkey and the Netherlands, and there are references to it in novels, songs and films, from Agatha Christie to Frank Zappa, and *A Nightmare On Elm Street*.

One, Two, Three, Four, Five

One, two, three, four, five,
Once I caught a fish alive,
Six, seven, eight, nine, ten,
Then I let it go again.

Why did you let it go?
Because it bit my finger so.
Which finger did it bite?
This little finger on the right.

I was taught this as a finger counting game, unaware of its long history. It appeared in *Mother Goose's Melody*, printed in London around 1765, when a hare rather than a fish was caught alive. The change to a fish seems to date from 1888 and the three versions Henry Bolton collected in America.

There Was an Old Woman: Once Upon a Time

Many nursery rhymes derive from longer ballads, originally cheaply printed on a 'broadside', or broadsheet – an early version of a magazine or newspaper, containing news, ballads, rhymes and sometimes woodcut illustrations. These were widely circulated and often displayed on tavern walls but few survive and the earliest printed versions we have are in the published anthologies. The innocent stories known today often hide morality tales or underlying political messages.

Aiken Drum

There was a man lived in the moon, lived in the
    moon, lived in the moon,
There was a man lived in the moon,
And his name was Aiken Drum;

And he played upon a ladle, a ladle, a ladle,
And he played upon a ladle,
And his name was Aiken Drum.

And his hat was made of good cream cheese, good
cream cheese, good cream cheese,
And his hat was made of good cream cheese,
And his name was Aiken Drum.

And his coat was made of good roast beef, good
roast beef, good roast beef,
And his coat was made of good roast beef,
And his name was Aiken Drum.

And his buttons were made of penny loaves, penny
loaves, penny loaves,
And his buttons were made of penny loaves,
And his name was Aiken Drum.

His waistcoat was made of crust of pies, crust of
pies, crust of pies,
His waistcoat was made of crust of pies,
And his name was Aiken Drum.

His breeches were made of haggis bags, haggis bags,
haggis bags,
His breeches were made of haggis bags,
And his name was Aiken Drum.

There was a man in another town, another town,
    another town,
There was a man in another town,
And his name was Willy Wood;

And he played upon a razor, a razor, a razor,
And he played upon a razor,
And his name was Willy Wood.

And he ate up all the good cream cheese, good
    cream cheese, good cream cheese,
And he ate up all the good cream cheese,
And his name was Willy Wood.

And he ate up all the good roast beef, good roast
    beef, good roast beef,
And he ate up all the good roast beef,
And his name was Willy Wood.

And he ate up all the penny loaves, penny loaves,
    penny loaves,
And he ate up all the penny loaves,
And his name was Willy Wood.

And he ate up all the good pie crust, good pie crust,
    good pie crust,
And he ate up all the good pie crust,
And his name was Willy Wood.

But he choked upon the haggis bags, haggis bags,
    haggis bags,
But he choked upon the haggis bags,
And that ended Willy Wood.

The rhyme was already popular in Scotland when it was published in James Hogg's *Jacobite Relics* in 1821. The name Aiken Drum seems to have been taken from a song about the battle of Sheriffmuir in 1715, at the height of the Jacobite Rebellion.

The Jacobite Rebellion

The Jacobites sought to restore the Stuarts to the throne of Britain after James II was deposed in 1688 and replaced by his daughter Mary II and her husband William III of Orange.

At the battle of Sheriffmuir on 13 November, John Erskine led the Highland chiefs for the Jacobite cause against British government forces led by the Duke of Argyll. The battle was inconclusive, with both sides claiming victory.

Other Aiken Drums

In his novel *The Antiquary*, Sir Walter Scott used the name for the bridegroom in the beggar Edie Ochiltree's story. It was also used by the poet William Nicholson for the faery or brownie in his poem of 1825. This led to suggestions that the name Aiken Drum may have come from older folklore but there is no evidence of the name's existence before the Jacobite song.

Cobbler, Cobbler, Mend My Shoe

> Cobbler, cobbler, mend my shoe,
> Get it done by half-past two;
> Half-past two is much too late,
> Get it done by half-past eight.
> Stitch it up, and stitch it down,
> And I'll give you half a crown.

Cobblers, though important craftsmen with their own guild of trade, were generally considered less skilled (or expensive) than shoemakers who worked with new leather to create bespoke shoes. Cobblers used old leather to make repairs, although they would sometimes take worn shoes apart to create a cheap 'new' shoe, which may be what the last lines are referring to. There are many ancient superstitions surrounding shoes, from it being bad luck to put shoes on a table to hiding children's shoes in chimneys or attics to ward away evil. It is interesting that unlike many other old crafts – Cooper, Miller, Baker, to name but a few – Cobbler has not become a very common surname.

Hark, Hark, the Dogs Do Bark

> Hark, hark, the dogs do bark,
> The beggars are coming to town,
> Some in rags and some in tags,
> And one in a velvet gown.

There are two main theories about the rhyme's origins: one suggests it is Tudor, dating back to Elizabethan times when the vast number of wandering vagabonds was seen as a real threat to law and order, and beggars were feared especially by those living in small towns and isolated hamlets. The second links the rhyme to William of Orange. It is thought that 'beggars' was an old nickname for the Dutch who arrived with William in 1688 when he took over the throne of England in the Glorious Revolution; the 'one in a velvet gown' may even have been William III himself.

If All the Seas Were One Sea

If all the seas were one sea,
What a great sea that would be!
If all the trees were one tree,
What a great tree that would be!
And if all the axes were one axe,
What a great axe that would be!
And if all the men were one man,
What a great man that would be!
And if the great man took the great axe,
And cut down the great tree,
And let it fall into the great sea,
What a splish-splash that would be!

'If All the Seas Were One Sea' first appeared in *The Nursery Rhymes of England* in 1842 by the Victorian collector of children's rhymes, James Orchard Halliwell. Nothing is known of its origins but it's easy to see why its moral tone would appeal to the nineteenth-century reader.

If All the World Were Paper

If all the world were paper,
And all the sea were ink,
If all the trees were bread and cheese,
What should we have to drink?

Although it appears to have a similar tone to 'If All the Seas', this rhyme is far older. It is the first verse of a longer poem published in 1641 in *Witt's Recreations*. But its roots go back further still.

There are parallels with eleventh- and twelfth-century Jewish and Christian odes and even with the end of the New Testament Gospel of St John. The imagery appears in the folk songs and traditional tales of many countries across Europe and the eastern Mediterranean, although the paper sometimes represents the heavens rather than the world.

Peter, Peter, Pumpkin Eater

> Peter, Peter, pumpkin eater,
> Had a wife and couldn't keep her;
> He put her in a pumpkin shell,
> And there he kept her very well.
>
> Peter, Peter, pumpkin eater,
> Had another, and didn't love her;
> Peter learned to read and spell,
> And then he loved her very well.

Not a great deal is known about this rhyme. Its first appearance in *Mother Goose's Quarto*, published in Boston, Massachusetts, around 1825, suggests it is of American origin, although there is a Scots version recorded later in the century with the first line, 'Peter my neeper', a reference to turnips or yellow swede.

It has also been suggested that Peter's wife was unfaithful and that a pumpkin shell was a euphemism for a chastity belt – that favoured medieval method of dealing with a potentially wayward wife.

The rhyme could also be seen to have a pro-education message. Once Peter had learned to read and write, his life seems to have become a whole lot better.

Rub-a-Dub-Dub, Three Men in a Tub

Rub-a-dub-dub, three men in a tub,
And who do you think they be?
The butcher, the baker, the candlestick-maker,
And all of them gone to sea.

Another version has the three jumping out of a rotten potato and early editions, published in *Christmas Box* in London in 1798, and *Mother Goose's Quarto* in Boston, Massachusetts, around 1825, have the same traders visiting a sideshow at a fair:

Rub-a-dub-dub, three maids in a tub,
And who do you think were there?
The butcher, the baker, the candlestick-maker,
And all of them gone to the fair.

Simple Simon Met a Pieman

Simple Simon met a pieman,
Going to the fair;
Says Simple Simon to the pieman,
'Let me taste your ware.'

Says the pieman to Simple Simon,
'Show me first your penny.'
Says Simple Simon to the pieman,
'Indeed I have not any.'

Simple Simon went a-fishing,
For to catch a whale;
All the water he had got,
Was in his mother's pail.

Simple Simon went to look
If plums grew on a thistle;
He pricked his fingers very much,
Which made poor Simon whistle.

He went for water with a sieve,
But soon it all ran through;
And now poor Simple Simon
Bids you all adieu.

The nursery rhyme we know was part of a chapbook called *Simple Simon*, printed in 1764. This in turn came from an older ballad, *Simple Simon's Misfortunes And His Wife*

Margery's Cruelty, which dates back at least to 1685 and possibly to Elizabethan times; the idea of Simon as a simpleton is even older. The French word 'adieu' was quite common in English from the early fourteenth century, and it appears in Chaucer's *Troilus and Cressida* around 1385. There is also a theory that the pieman was King James I, who sold honours and titles in exchange for contributions to the royal treasury.

There Was a Crooked Man

There was a crooked man, and he walked a crooked mile,
He found a crooked sixpence against a crooked stile,
He bought a crooked cat, which caught a crooked mouse,
And they all lived together in a little crooked house.

Crooked in this context means dishonest or disloyal, and the 'crooked man' is said to be Sir Alexander Leslie, the Scottish general who led the Covenanters and Scottish army in the reign of Charles I. He also fought for the Dutch and Swedish armies, and switched allegiance constantly, amassing a fortune in the process, as well as accepting a peerage from the king – 'a crooked sixpence'. After the Solemn League and Covenant was signed binding the parliaments of England and Scotland, Sir Leslie marched or 'walked a crooked mile' from Edinburgh to the Scottish border, 'the crooked stile', and defeated the Royalists at Marston Moor in 1644. The Scottish Army may be the 'crooked cat' and the battle the 'crooked mouse'. He later handed Charles I over to the English Parliamentarians, who executed the king. Against all odds, the alliance between the two countries held, creating the 'crooked house'.

A grand story for such a simple-sounding rhyme, although it did not appear in print until James Orchard Halliwell recorded it in the 1840s and so there is no real way of knowing whether or not it is true.

There Was a Little Girl Who Had a Little Curl

There was a little girl who had a little curl,
Right in the middle of her forehead.
And when she was good, she was very, very good,
But when she was bad, she was horrid.

There is some question about the origins of this rhyme, but the usual and best story is that it was written by Henry Wadsworth Longfellow in the 1850s, composed on the spur of the moment for his baby daughter, Edith. His son Ernest describes him walking up and down, cradling Edith, singing it to her. Extra verses are sometimes added but there has never been any suggestion that Longfellow also wrote those.

There Was an Old Woman Tossed Up in a Basket

There was an old woman tossed up in a basket,
Seventeen times as high as the moon;
Where she was going I couldn't but ask it,
For in her hand she carried a broom.
'Old woman, old woman, old woman,' quoth I,
'Where are you going to up so high?'
'To brush the cobwebs off the sky!'
'May I go with you?'
'Aye, by and by.'

Old women are a popular feature in nursery rhymes and this
one seems to be particularly old. The verse appeared in one
of the earliest anthologies, *Mother Goose's Melody*, around

37

1765, where it was claimed that the old woman was Henry V. There are also associations with another king, James II, probably because it is sung to the tune of 'Lilliburlero' (you can listen on YouTube), which is said to have 'danced James II out of three kingdoms'. According to Samuel Johnson, the song was a favourite of the playwright Oliver Goldsmith, although at the time the old woman was 'toss'd in a blanket' and ninety-nine times as high as the moon.

There Was an Old Woman Who Lived in a Shoe

There was an old woman who lived in a shoe,
She had so many children, she didn't know what to do;
She gave them some broth without any bread,
Then whipped them all soundly, and put them to bed.

The two main contenders for the identity of the old woman are Queen Caroline, wife of George II, who had eight children, and Elizabeth Vergoose of Boston, who had six children of her own and a further ten stepchildren, but this seems to be for no real reason other than their large families. (Elizabeth Vergoose is also sometimes claimed to be the inspiration for Mother Goose.) King George II has also been suggested because he led the fashion for wearing white powdered wigs and was referred to derisively as the old woman, the children being the MPs, and England the shoe.

It was first published in *Gammer Gurton's Garland* in 1794 with a different final line: 'She whipp'd all their bums, and sent them to bed.' And Iona and Peter Opie, the renowned collectors of children's stories and rhymes, were struck by the Shakespearean term 'a-loffeing' which appears at the end of the *Infant Institutes* version in 1797:

Then out went th' old woman to bespeak 'em a
  coffin,
And when she came back she found 'em all
  a-loffeing.

They suggested the rhyme could be far older than the earliest printed examples and might have origins in folklore, especially as shoes were traditionally linked to marriage and fertility.

This is the House That Jack Built

This is the house that Jack built.

This is the malt
That lay in the house that Jack built.

This is the rat,
That ate the malt
That lay in the house that Jack built.

This is the cat,
That killed the rat,
That ate the malt
That lay in the house that Jack built.

This is the dog,
That worried the cat,
That killed the rat,
That ate the malt
That lay in the house that Jack built.

This is the cow with the crumpled horn,
That tossed the dog,
That worried the cat,
That killed the rat,
That ate the malt
That lay in the house that Jack built.

This is the maiden all forlorn,
That milked the cow with the crumpled horn,
That tossed the dog,
That worried the cat,
That killed the rat,
That ate the malt
That lay in the house that Jack built.

This is the man all tattered and torn,
That kissed the maiden all forlorn,
That milked the cow with the crumpled horn,
That tossed the dog,

That worried the cat,
That killed the rat,
That ate the malt
That lay in the house that Jack built.

This is the priest all shaven and shorn,
That married the man all tattered and torn,
That kissed the maiden all forlorn,
That milked the cow with the crumpled horn,
That tossed the dog,
That worried the cat,
That killed the rat,
That ate the malt
That lay in the house that Jack built.

This is the cock that crowed in the morn,
That waked the priest all shaven and shorn,
That married the man all tattered and torn,
That kissed the maiden all forlorn,
That milked the cow with the crumpled horn,
That tossed the dog,
That worried the cat,
That killed the rat,
That ate the malt
That lay in the house that Jack built.

This is the farmer sowing his corn,
That kept the cock that crowed in the morn,
That waked the priest all shaven and shorn,
That married the man all tattered and torn,

That kissed the maiden all forlorn,
That milked the cow with the crumpled horn,
That tossed the dog,
That worried the cat,
That killed the rat,
That ate the malt
That lay in the house that Jack built.

This is the horse and the hound and the horn,
That belonged to the farmer sowing his corn,
That kept the cock that crowed in the morn,
That waked the priest all shaven and shorn,
That married the man all tattered and torn,
That kissed the maiden all forlorn,
That milked the cow with the crumpled horn,
That tossed the dog,
That worried the cat,
That killed the rat,
That ate the malt
That lay in the house that Jack built.

This nursery rhyme was originally printed by John Newbery around 1750 and was an immediate hit. Much copied, it inspired pantomimes and parodies poking fun at everyone from architects to politicians, and even Napoleon Bonaparte. Since it first appeared, there has been speculation about its meaning with several books devoted to the subject, but there are few facts.

A Jewish Aramaic chant that was printed in Prague in 1590 has been suggested to have inspired the rhyme, but although the chant is also a cumulative tale, the contents are very different.

James Orchard Halliwell pointed to the 'priest all shaven and shorn' as evidence that the rhyme must date back at least to the mid-sixteenth century and the fact that versions of the rhyme exist in most European languages also suggests it is fairly old.

Cherrington Manor in Shropshire, which once had a malt house in its grounds, is sometimes said to be the original house that Jack built.

Where Are You Going to, My Pretty Maid?

> Where are you going to, my pretty maid?
> I'm going a-milking, sir, she said,
> Sir, she said, sir, she said,
> I'm going a-milking, sir, she said.
> May I go with you, my pretty maid?
> You're kindly welcome, sir, she said.
> Say, will you marry me, my pretty maid?
> Yes, if you please, kind sir, she said.
> What is your father, my pretty maid?
> My father's a farmer, sir, she said.
> What is your fortune, my pretty maid?

My face is my fortune, sir, she said.
Then I can't marry you, my pretty maid.
Nobody asked you, sir, she said.

This is an example of the Victorians taking an older folk song and sanitizing it for the nursery. At a time when childhood didn't really exist for most children, an idealized vision of children's innocence was being created.

The reality was very different. Although child-labour reforms such as the 1833 Factory Act and Mines Act of 1841 began to restrict the use of young children in dangerous jobs, life was still very hard for the majority. By 1860, it is estimated that only around a half of all children between five and fifteen had any regular schooling.

'Where Are You Going to, My Pretty Maid?' was a popular seventeenth-century folk song, the original lyrics being far more explicit and adult. The form it takes with the man and the maid answering one another is similar to medieval French troubadours' ballads.

Monday's Child: The Rhythm of Days

There are many ancient superstitions connected to the days of the week and seasons. So-called fortune rhymes often feature births, deaths and marriages and were perhaps an attempt to exert some control in what must have seemed a very unpredictable world. Alongside these, nursery rhymes have always celebrated festivals, with Christmas a particular favourite.

Christmas is Coming

Christmas is coming, and the goose is getting fat,
Please put a penny in the old man's hat;
If you haven't a penny, a ha'penny will do,
If you haven't a ha'penny, then God bless you!

This is a well-known Christmas nursery rhyme, probably dating back to the nineteenth century and a time when geese were the cheaper and more common choice for the Christmas feast. It's a reminder to be charitable and was popularized in the 1950s by the singers Bing Crosby and Harry Belafonte, and later as a calypso by John Denver and the Muppets.

Monday's Child is Fair of Face

Monday's child is fair of face,
Tuesday's child is full of grace,
Wednesday's child is full of woe,
Thursday's child has far to go,
Friday's child is loving and giving,
Saturday's child works hard for a living,
And the child that is born on the Sabbath day,
Is bonny and blithe, and good and gay.

The idea of Sunday as an auspicious day on which to be born goes back to the Middle Ages; whether this rhyme is as old as that is debateable but it does seem to be part of an ancient tradition of fortune-telling proverbs. The Elizabethan writer Thomas Nashe refers to the faiths and fables of his childhood growing up in Suffolk in the 1570s, and this rhyme is likely to be one of several versions circulating before this time. Prince Charles's birth in 1948 sparked a heated debate in Parliament and the press about the correct wording.

Thomas Nashe also wrote advising which days were best to cut your nails:

Cut Your Nails Monday

Cut your nails Monday, you cut them for news,
Cut them on Tuesday, a pair of new shoes,
Cut them on Wednesday, you cut them for health,
Cut them on Thursday, 'twill add to your wealth,
Cut them on Friday, you cut them for woe,
Cut them on Saturday, a journey you'll go,
Cut them on Sunday, you cut them for evil,
All the week long you'll be ruled by the devil.

Cutting a baby's nails before she was a year old was said to bring bad luck and make the child light-fingered. Mothers would chew their baby's nails instead.

Sneezes, too, were seen as highly significant:

Sneeze on Monday

Sneeze on Monday, sneeze for danger,
Sneeze on Tuesday, kiss a stranger,
Sneeze on Wednesday, receive a letter,

Sneeze on Thursday, something better,
Sneeze on Friday, sneeze for sorrow,
Sneeze on Saturday, meet your sweetheart tomorrow,
Sneeze on Sunday, your safety seek,
The devil will have you for the rest of the week.

This last links with the superstition that sneezes were omens, associated with evil – either the body trying to rid itself of evil, or bad spirits waiting to leap in. The custom of saying 'God bless you' after a sneeze is universal across cultures.

Remember, Remember, the Fifth of November

Remember, remember, the fifth of November,
Gunpowder, treason, and plot;
I see no reason why gunpowder treason,
Should ever be forgot.

There is no mystery surrounding the origin of this verse: it commemorates the foiled Gunpowder Plot by Guy Fawkes and twelve others to blow up Parliament in 1605. Guy Fawkes was caught guarding the barrels of gunpowder and was hung, drawn and quartered for his crime. The following year,

Parliament commissioned a sermon to remember the event and to act as a warning to any would-be plotters. It is still celebrated in the UK each year on 5 November with fireworks and bonfires on which effigies of the 'guy' are burned.

Solomon Grundy

> Solomon Grundy,
> Born on Monday,
> Christened on Tuesday,
> Married on Wednesday,
> Took ill on Thursday,
> Worse on Friday,
> Died on Saturday,
> Buried on Sunday,
> This is the end
> Of Solomon Grundy.

This rhyme appeared in Halliwell's nursery rhyme book of 1842 when it was already well known; it probably evolved as a way of teaching children the days of the week. Rather disappointingly there is no evidence that it was ever based on a real person, though I really feel it should have been. For many people now, Solomon Grundy is better known as the zombie supervillain in DC Comics, introduced as an adversary of the Green Lantern in 1944.

Thirty Days Hath September

> Thirty days hath September,
> April, June, and November;
> All the rest have thirty-one,
> Excepting February alone,
> Which has twenty-eight days clear,
> And twenty-nine in each leap year.

Versions of this verse were quoted by Elizabethan writers but it was first recorded earlier in thirteenth-century France. Its origins may be traced even further back to the Julian calendar, introduced by Julius Caesar in 46 BC, which set out the basic system of four months of thirty days, seven thirty-one-day months, and one twenty-eight-day month with an extra day added each leap year (originally every third year). It is still the mnemonic most children learn to remember the number of days in each month.

Humpty Dumpty: Royal Connections

People generally love gossip and there has always been a demand for royal gossip, although in past times to be caught spreading salacious stories about the royals or other eminent figures could have dire consequences. As a result, true identities were often hidden behind apparently innocent verses. Richard III, Elizabeth I, the other Tudor monarchs and their Stuart successors were particularly popular subjects.

Humpty Dumpty

> Humpty Dumpty sat on a wall,
> Humpty Dumpty had a great fall.
> All the king's horses,
> And all the king's men,
> Couldn't put Humpty together again.

The image of Humpty Dumpty as an egg is so familiar that we usually forget that the rhyme was originally meant as a riddle. It is ancient and there are versions in many other countries including '*Boule, boule*' in France, '*Thille Lille*' in Sweden and '*Lille-Trille*' in Denmark, and '*Runtzelken-Puntzelken*' or '*Humpelken-Pumpelken*' in Germany.

There have been many theories about its origins, including the idea that Humpty Dumpty was King Richard III of England, or that it was a piece of military weaponry used during the English Civil War: either a siege engine called a 'tortoise', or a powerful cannon positioned on top of the church tower of St Mary-At-The-Walls in Colchester by Royalists to fire on the Parliamentarians.

Humpty Dumpty was also the name of a boiled brandy and ale drink in the seventeenth century, according to the *Oxford English Dictionary*. Several nineteenth-century American writers describe a girls' game called Humpty Dumpty in which girls sit in a circle holding their skirts around their feet. At a signal they fall backwards and must sit up again without letting go of their skirts. Linguistic experts believe the rhyme is likely to predate all these stories.

I Had a Little Nut Tree

I had a little nut tree,
Nothing would it bear,
But a silver nutmeg
And a golden pear.

The King of Spain's daughter
Came to visit me,
And all for the sake
Of my little nut tree.

I skipped over the water,
I danced over the sea,
And all the birds in the air
Couldn't catch me.

This was the version I loved as a child but the third verse is not always included and may be an eighteenth-century addition. There are also two extra verses about the King of Spain's daughter but these are more recent:

Her dress was made of crimson,
Jet black was her hair,
She asked me for my nut tree
And my golden pear.

I said, 'So fair a princess
Never did I see,
I'll give you all the fruit
From my little nut tree.'

'I Had a Little Nut Tree' first appeared in print around 1797 in a book called *Newest Christmas Box*, but it is likely to be far older in origin. A collection of songs and carols dating from around 1440 includes something remarkably similar.

A Fair Princess

The King of Spain's daughter appears regularly in romantic songs and rhymes throughout Europe from the early sixteenth century, and is usually thought to be Juana of Castile, more often referred to as 'Juana the Mad'.

Juana, who lived from 1479 to 1555, was the first queen to reign over both Castile and Aragon in Spain. She also ruled the kingdoms of Naples, Sicily and Sardinia along with a vast empire in the relatively newly discovered Americas.

Her story was not a happy one and whether she was mad for love or a victim of political power play is not clear. Two years before she inherited the throne of Castile she seems to have become mentally imbalanced, consumed by jealousy over her husband, Philip the Handsome of Burgundy. The pair were married in 1496 and Juana bore him six children, ensuring the future of Habsburg rule in Spain. Over the next half-century, Juana's husband, father and son all ruled as regent in her place, confining poor Juana to a convent for most of her long life. Her mental illness – whether depression, psychosis or schizophrenia – was no doubt not helped by her enforced confinement in a windowless room. But as the devoted, faithful wife of a philandering husband, Juana captured the public's imagination and has been immortalized in rhyme, song and art.

At the English Court

Juana is known to have visited Henry VII's court in 1506, which may have inspired the nursery rhyme, especially as Henry was said to be keen to marry her following the deaths of both his queen, Elizabeth, and Juana's husband, Philip. He reluctantly conceded that his advisors were right: though capable of providing him with healthy heirs, Juana was undoubtedly not of sound mind and so marriage might not be wise. At the time, Juana was refusing to allow her dead husband's embalmed body to be entombed.

It is just possible that the princess in the rhyme could have been Juana's younger sister, Catherine of Aragon, who became the first wife of Henry VIII. Catherine was popular with the English people, who generally distrusted her successor, Anne Boleyn.

Though both the Spanish king's daughters were considered fair of face, neither had jet black hair. Portraits and accounts from the time describe them as having reddish-blonde or auburn hair.

Old King Cole

Old King Cole was a merry old soul,
And a merry old soul was he;
He called for his pipe,
And he called for his bowl,
And he called for his fiddlers three.

Every fiddler, he had a fiddle,
And a very fine fiddle had he;
Oh, there's none so rare,
As can compare,
With King Cole and his fiddlers three.

The roots of the rhyme may lie far back in Roman Britain, with two possible candidates for King Cole.

Coel, Coel or Cole?

The first contender is Coel the Magnificent, a third-century prince of Colchester. Geoffrey of Monmouth favours this idea in his twelfth-century chronicle, but he is notoriously unreliable. He has it that Coel's daughter, Helena, was an accomplished musician. Helena became the consort of the emperor Constantius and mother of Constantine the Great. A devout Christian, she is said to have found the relics of the True Cross.

The second Cole is Coel Hen, whose name can be translated as 'the old'. He ruled northern Britain in the fourth century when the Romans were withdrawing back to mainland Europe. He was possibly the last Roman ruler in the region and is thought to have fathered many children, and, in the process, a number of ruling dynasties.

Alternatively, Cole may have been a twelfth-century cloth merchant from Reading named Thomas Cole-Brook. A man of great wealth and influence, he was a well-known figure in Restoration plays.

A Merry Old Soul

The pipe in the rhyme could refer to a recorder or flute-like musical instrument that King Cole played along with his fiddlers, but it may equally be a smoking pipe for the king to sit back and enjoy along with his bowl of ale while his musicians entertained.

Pussycat, Pussycat, Where Have You Been?

> Pussycat, pussycat, where have you been?
> I've been to London to look at the queen.
> Pussycat, pussycat, what did you there?
> I frightened a little mouse under the chair.

The queen is Elizabeth I and the rhyme is said to describe a real incident at Windsor Castle when a cat belonging to one of the ladies-in-waiting chased a mouse beneath Elizabeth's chair, brushing against the queen's leg and startling her. It has occasionally been suggested that the queen is actually Caroline of Brunswick, wife of George IV, and that the verse is a parody of the parties she regularly held.

There is also a rather delightful story connected to the rhyme showing the lighter side of Queen Victoria. When politician Lord Ernle was due to visit the queen at Osborne House, his daughter asked for the little mouse that lived under her chair. Victoria was very amused by this but one of her elderly advisors remained puzzled, whereupon the queen turned to him and recited the nursery rhyme as explanation.

The Grand Old Duke of York

> Oh the grand old Duke of York,
> He had ten thousand men;
> He marched them up to the top of the hill,
> And he marched them down again.
>
> And when they were up, they were up,
> And when they were down, they were down,

> And when they were only halfway up,
> They were neither up nor down.

The rhyme is very similar to 'The King Of France Went Up The Hill With Forty Thousand Men' and as it is usually sung to an old French air it is probable that the words were simply adapted from the French at some point.

There are various possibilities for the identity of the duke.

Which Duke?

Harking back to the Wars of the Roses, he could be Richard, 3rd Duke of York, who was defeated and killed at the Battle of Wakefield on 30 December 1460. Richard was waiting for reinforcements at Sandal Castle, when the hill on which it stood was surrounded by Lancastrian troops. He decided to charge into battle with only a reduced army and lost the fight.

Unpopular King James II, also Duke of York, is another candidate. He marched his army to Salisbury Plain to resist the invasion by his son-in-law William III, only to retreat without fighting.

The character most often linked to the rhyme is eighteenth-century Prince Frederick, Duke of York and second son of George III. He was commander-in-chief of British troops during the Napoleonic Wars and following a defeat in the Flanders Campaign he was recalled to London. Though Flanders is generally flat, the town of Cassel is built on a small hill, which could be the hill in question.

The Queen of Hearts

The Queen of Hearts
She made some tarts,
All on a summer's day;
The Knave of Hearts
He stole the tarts,
And took them clean away.

The King of Hearts
Called for the tarts,
And beat the Knave full sore;
The Knave of Hearts
Brought back the tarts,
And vowed he'd steal no more.

Lewis Carroll famously included the Queen of Hearts in *Alice In Wonderland*, first published in 1865. Carroll's Queen is said to be a caricature of Queen Victoria but the character predates this. The twelve-line rhyme appeared with verses about the King of Clubs, the King of Spades and the Diamond King, in *The European Magazine* of 1782 but the Queen of Hearts was always the most popular and the other verses have largely been forgotten. Iona and Peter Opie, renowned folklorists and collectors of children's rhymes, stories and games, argue convincingly that the Queen of Hearts rhyme is also much older than the others.

French playing cards from 1650 depict the Queen of Hearts as Judith, who beheaded the Assyrian general Holofernes in the biblical Book of Judith, saving her home city of Bethulia and its inhabitants. In the original English playing-card deck, the Queen of Hearts is supposed to represent Elizabeth of York, wife and queen of Henry VII. It is sometimes suggested that Elizabeth of Bohemia was the original inspiration for the character. Elizabeth was the daughter of James I of England and VI of Scotland. She married Frederick V who was briefly king of Bohemia and she is sometimes known as the Winter Queen. Her descendants went on to become the Hanoverian rulers of Great Britain.

William and Mary, George and Anne

> William and Mary, George and Anne,
> Four such children had never a man:
> They put their father to flight and shame,
> And called their brother a shocking bad name.

Written about James II's two daughters Mary and Anne and their respective husbands, William of Orange and George of Denmark, this nursery rhyme probably comes from a ballad written just after the Glorious Revolution of 1688. Protestant Mary and Anne were James's only surviving children from his first marriage to Lady Anne Hyde.

There was no love lost between their husbands, who represented the rival Anglo-Dutch and Anglo-Danish alliances.

James II had become increasingly unpopular through his pro-French, pro-Catholic stance, and was distrusted for his belief in the divine right of kings and absolute monarchy. Matters grew more serious after the death of Lady Anne, when James married Mary of Modena and openly converted to Catholicism. The birth of a Catholic heir was the final blow, and William of Orange, who was not only James's son-in-law but also his nephew, was asked to lead an invasion army in 1688. James's flight to France was taken to signal his abdication and the English Bill of Rights was passed appointing William and Mary joint king and queen.

James II lived out his days at the French court of Louis XIV. His son, also named James, was smuggled out of England to live in exile with his parents. James went on to claim the British throne on the death of his father in 1701 and led the first of the Jacobite rebellions. He became known as the Old Pretender, while his son, Bonnie Prince Charlie, was the Young Pretender.

Little Bo-Peep: Old Friends

It is often impossible to know the true identity of the person behind the rhyme. There are many conflicting stories which might all be true, at least in part. Even today, nursery rhymes are appropriated and adapted: with a few tweaks, the same verse could apply to several different people or events. The mystery surrounding them seems to add to their charm.

Curly Locks

Curly Locks, Curly Locks,
Wilt thou be mine?
Thou shalt not wash dishes,
Nor yet feed the swine,
But sit on a cushion,
And sew a fine seam,

> And feed upon strawberries,
> Sugar, and cream.

There are various versions dating back at least to 1797 including 'Pussycat, pussycat, wilt thou be mine?' and 'Bonny lass, bonny lass'. It may be that the words were changed in the nineteenth century when curly hair was seen as particularly attractive. Tradition has it that Curly Locks was Charles II, although there is no firm evidence for this.

Daffy-Down-Dilly

> Daffy-Down-Dilly is new come to town,
> With a yellow petticoat, and a green gown.

These lines were printed in *Songs for the Nursery* in 1805 but the term 'daffy-down-dilly' was an older colloquial name for a daffodil. The poet and farmer Thomas Tusser used it in *Five Hundred Points Of Good Husbandry* in 1573. This long poem of rhyming couplets provides a fascinating insight into Tudor life and customs, including instructions, and recording proverbs and dialect phrases.

Diddle, Diddle, Dumpling, My Son John

Diddle, diddle, dumpling, my son John,
Went to bed with his trousers on,
One shoe off, and one shoe on,
Diddle, diddle, dumpling, my son John.

Hot dumpling sellers in the streets of old London would have been heard calling 'Diddle, diddle, dumpling' to advertise their wares. This is one of the few nursery rhymes to use the name John rather than its alternative, Jack, and it was first recorded in *The Newest Christmas Box*, printed in London around 1797.

It seems to have been a favourite of the early nineteenth-century essayist and writer Charles Lamb, and Keats refers to the rhyme in his unfinished poem 'The Cap And Bells'. It was made famous again in the early twentieth century by the music-hall entertainer Arthur Lloyd.

Doctor Foster Went to Gloucester

Doctor Foster went to Gloucester
In a shower of rain;
He stepped in a puddle,
Right up to his middle,
And never went there again.

In his *Mother Goose* anthology of 1919, Boyd Smith suggested that Doctor Foster was Edward I. The English king reigned from 1272 to 1307 and was famous for his castle building in the Welsh Marches. Standing over six feet tall, he was nicknamed 'Longshanks' due to his unusual height, and was an imposing character. Having conquered Wales in the 1280s, he turned his attention towards Scotland with rather less success.

The nursery rhyme is said to record a visit Edward made to the city of Gloucester during a particularly rainy season. His horse became stuck in the mud, forcing the king to dismount into a muddy puddle or stream. So humiliated was he, that he vowed never to return. Gloucester was also the scene of the opening battle of the Second Baron's War (1264–7), which Edward successfully won, retaking the city from Simon de Montfort's forces.

Whether true or not, it's a good story and the rhyming of puddle with middle suggests that the verse dates back to old English when 'piddle' was the usual form of the word puddle, meaning stream.

Edward's campaigns against Scotland are reflected in another rhyme occasionally remembered in Scotland. It dates from the time of the siege of Berwick in 1296 and is said to have been very unpopular with the king:

> Kyng Edward,
> When thou havest Beric,
> Pike thee!

When thou havest geton,
Dike thee!

Georgie Porgie, Pudding and Pie

Georgie Porgie, pudding and pie,
Kissed the girls and made them cry;
When the boys came out to play,
Georgie Porgie ran away.

For a long time I was under the impression that Georgie Porgie was the Prince Regent, later George IV (1762–1830), and that the verse reflected his gluttony extravagance and general unpopularity. But the nursery rhyme is very widely known and there are a number of different suggestions for Georgie's true identity.

The Real Georgie Porgie

One of the most popular candidates is George Villiers, 1st Duke of Buckingham (1592–1628). He seems to have been quite a character. He was the lover of King James I who nicknamed him 'Steenie', a reference to St Stephen who is described in the Bible as having the face of an angel. Villiers had numerous other lovers, including Anne of Austria with whom he had a lengthy affair; Anne was Queen of France and wife of Louis XIII. The pair's private liaisons and political scheming feature in Dumas' *The Three Musketeers*.

The other main contenders are George I and Charles II, who was popularly known as the Merrie Monarch, a reference to the hedonism and frivolity of his court. He most certainly 'kissed the girls' – although he had no legitimate heirs, he acknowledged at least fourteen illegitimate children by different mistresses. Another of his nicknames was 'Old Rowley' and this rhyme may have started out as, 'Rowley, Powley, pudding and pie'.

In 1841, *The Kentish Coronal* (a book of prose and poetry connected to Kent) was obviously very familiar with the nursery rhyme, using it to satirize poetry critics of the time. It asserted that Georgie Porgie was 'a celebrated character, who existed in the reign of the Emperor Charlemagne.'

Jack and Jill

Jack and Jill went up the hill
To fetch a pail of water;
Jack fell down and broke his crown,
And Jill came tumbling after.

Up Jack got, and home did trot,
As fast as he could caper;
He went to bed to mend his head,
With vinegar and brown paper.

Jack is the name that appears most often in nursery rhymes, perhaps because it was used as a general 'everyman's' name while Jill was taken to mean any young girl or sweetheart from the Middle Ages; Shakespeare used the names in this context in both *Love's Labour's Lost* and *A Midsummer Night's Dream* where he wrote, 'Jack shall have Jill; nought shall go ill', and there is a proverb which claims 'A good Jack makes a good Jill'.

Analysing the language, the Opies suggest the rhyming of 'water' with 'after' would date the nursery rhyme to the beginning of the seventeenth century. Others focus on the oddness of going up a hill to fetch water, although wells are sometimes found on high ground and defensive castles, often built on hills or mounds, usually had a water source within their walls.

Hjuki and Bil

Water is traditionally associated with many ancient superstitions and water rhymes often have a long history. One theory traces the origins of 'Jack and Jill' to the Norse myths. Two children, Hjuki and Bil, were walking home one evening after drawing water from a well when they were captured by Mani, the moon. According to legend, the children can still be seen when the moon is full, with the bucket hanging from a pole between them. It's not hard to see that Hjuki, which is pronounced Juki in Norse, could easily become Jack, and Bil could be feminized to Jill; in fact, an early woodcut illustration for the rhyme shows the children as two boys.

Other Theories

John Bellenden Ker, a Victorian botanist, wrote four books about nursery rhymes, arguing that they were all written in 'low Saxon' and were anti-clerical in meaning. He put forward the idea that Jack and Jill were really two priests. A century later, Katherine Elwes developed this idea to suggest that Jack was Cardinal Wolsey and Jill was Bishop Tarbes, the cleric responsible for negotiating the political marriage between Mary Tudor, the younger sister of Henry VIII, and Louis XII of France.

There are other stories, including a theory that the rhyme reflects Charles I's attempts to reform taxes on liquid measures – Jill being 'gill', a quarter-pint measure. It has even been suggested that Jack and Jill represent the French King Louis XVI and Queen Marie Antoinette, guillotined during the French Revolution in 1793.

A Folk Remedy

'Vinegar and brown paper' is a standard old remedy for headaches and bruises – the vinegar helping to draw out the bruise – but it is possible that this second verse was a later addition.

There are also other verses that appear particularly in nineteenth-century nursery-rhyme collections. The best known is:

Then Jill came in,
And she did grin,
To see Jack's paper plaster;
Her mother whipt her,
Across her knee,
For laughing at Jack's disaster.

Jack Be Nimble

Jack be nimble,
Jack be quick,
Jack jump over
The candlestick.

This is another rhyme that is linked to fortune-telling. It recalls an old English practice of candle-leaping which was especially popular at Christmas time and at weddings. A lit candle was placed on the floor and if it stayed alight when someone jumped over the flame, it signified they would have good luck all year. The tradition was particularly associated with lace-makers, although there are records of it still taking place in Suffolk pubs at the start of the twentieth century. Alternately, the rhyme could be about a sixteenth-century English pirate known as Black Jack. He was reputed to be very nimble when it came to avoiding capture.

Jack Sprat

> Jack Sprat could eat no fat,
> His wife could eat no lean,
> And so between them both you see,
> They licked the platter clean.

This simple little verse has a long history. It was first recorded by botanist and traveller John Ray in his 1670 catalogue of English proverbs, but there are references to it in other books at least a century earlier. Jack Sprat was a slang term for someone who was a dwarf in the sixteenth and seventeenth centuries.

There are various theories on who might have inspired the character. One is that Jack Sprat was Charles I, left 'lean' when Parliament refused to raise taxes to finance his support for Louis XIII against the French Protestant Huguenots. Measuring 5 feet 4 inches, Charles was painfully aware of his short stature and was painted on horseback by Anthony Van Dyck to give him the appearance of height. His wife, Henrietta Maria, was French, a Catholic, hardly spoke English, and remained unpopular with the nation, especially when she appeared to be meddling in affairs of state.

Or it could refer to twelfth-century Richard I, the Lionheart, and his avaricious, generally disliked brother John, of Magna Carta fame. While journeying back from the Third Crusade, Richard was captured by Duke Leopold of Austria. While his mother, Eleanor of Aquitaine, raised the £70,000 ransom demanded, brother John set about seizing the throne. The rhyme has also been linked to the legend of Robin Hood, again involving greedy King John and the more heroic King Richard.

Little Bo-Peep

Little Bo-Peep has lost her sheep,
And doesn't know where to find them;
Leave them alone, and they'll come home,
Bringing their tails behind them.

Little Bo-Peep fell fast asleep,
And dreamt she heard them bleating;
But when she awoke, she found it a joke,
For they were still a'fleeting.

Then up she took her little crook,
Determined for to find them;
She found them indeed, but it made her heart bleed,
For they'd left their tails behind them.

It happened one day, as Bo-Peep did stray,
Into a meadow hard by;
There she espied their tails side by side,
All hung on a tree to dry.

She heaved a sigh, and wiped her eye,
And over the hillocks went rambling;
She tried what she could, as a shepherdess should,
To tack again each to its lambkin.

A child's game of hide and seek links the name Bo-Peep back to the Middle Ages and some lines are very similar to an early eighteenth-century version of 'Yankee Doodle'.

It is sometimes seen as a representation of the life of Mary Queen of Scots. The queen lost many of her supporters following her second marriage to Lord Darnley, who was murdered in suspicious circumstances, and throughout her life she remained the focus of great intrigue. However, there is a real lack of evidence to support this theory.

Now landlocked, the village of Ninfield in East Sussex was once at the centre of a notorious smuggling trade. Boats used to navigate the narrow waterways across the marshes led by Bo-Peep's sheep, so it is claimed. Again, firm evidence is missing.

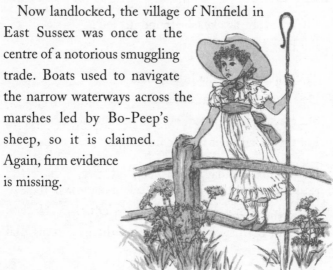

Little Boy Blue

Little Boy Blue,
Come blow your horn,
The sheep's in the meadow,
The cow's in the corn.

But where is the boy who looks after the sheep?
He's under the haystack, fast asleep.
Will you wake him? No, not I,
For if I do, he's sure to cry.

Tradition has it that the rhyme parodies the life of Cardinal Wolsey, Archbishop of York and Lord Chancellor to King Henry VIII.

Thomas Wolsey was probably born in 1475 and grew up in Ipswich. The son of a butcher, he may well have tended his father's animals as a boy. It was usual for butchers of this period to keep their own herds. Wolsey was a brilliant scholar, earning a degree from Oxford at the age of fifteen, and going on to become a noted statesman. Despite handing over his new palace at Hampton Court to Henry VIII, Wolsey fell from favour. He disapproved of the king's divorce from Catherine of Aragon and remarriage to Anne Boleyn, and paid dearly for his criticism. He was arrested for high treason and died on the way to his trial in 1530.

Whether or not Wolsey really inspired the rhyme is impossible to say for certain, but it appeared in *Tommy Thumb's Little Song Book* around 1744 and is probably much older. It may well be Tudor in origin and Shakespeare is possibly referring to it in *King Lear* when Edgar, masquerading as mad Tom, says:

> Sleepest or wakest thou, jolly shepheard?
> Thy sheepe be in the corne;
> And for one blast of thy minkin mouth
> Thy sheepe shall take no harme.

Although the nursery rhyme itself is less well known among children today, the title has had a lasting appeal. A. A. Milne wrote a poem called 'Little Bo-Peep and Little Boy Blue' in *When We Were Very Young*. Mick Jagger and Keith Richards' first group was called 'Little Boy Blue and the Blue Boys', and it continues to feature in a number of films, songs, books and comics.

Little Jack Horner

> Little Jack Horner sat in a corner,
> Eating a Christmas pie;
> He put in a thumb, and pulled out a plum,
> And said what a good boy am I!

An intriguing tale of treachery and deceit lies behind this innocent-sounding rhyme. Also said to date back to Tudor times and the days of Henry VIII, and in this case the story might just be true.

Following his break with Rome over his divorce and marriage to Anne Boleyn, Henry VIII passed the Act of Supremacy in 1534, establishing the Church of England and declaring himself the supreme head. Catholics were removed from office, their lands and property confiscated. The dissolution of the monasteries was the next step, with Henry and his chief adviser, Thomas Cromwell, seeking to redirect their wealth and income to the Crown. Monasteries were sacked and burned, the monks killed or forced to flee.

A Special Pie

At the beginning of 1539, Glastonbury Abbey was the only remaining monastery in Somerset; it was also one of the richest in Henry's kingdom. Perhaps hoping to appease the king, Richard Whiting, the last Abbott of Glastonbury, sent his steward Jack Horner to Henry's court with a specially baked Christmas pie in which were hidden the deeds to twelve prime manors owned by the abbey in Somerset. Hiding valuables in this way was not unusual at the time to protect them from highwaymen and robbers. Piecrusts were viewed as containers, not necessarily to be eaten. Some even included ingredients like sawdust to make them stronger.

Mells Manor

It is said that on the journey, Horner opened the pie and pulled out the title deeds to the Manor of Mells. As well as being the best, or plum, estate, the manor included lead mines in the Mendip Hills, the Latin word for lead being *plumbum*. Shortly after this date, a Thomas Horner is known to have taken possession of Mells, his descendants continuing to live there for over four hundred years.

The Horner family argue that Thomas Horner bought the manor for cash, possibly from the king's commissioners. They also stress that their ancestor was Thomas, not Jack, but then at that time any man might be called Jack, especially if he was regarded as something of a lad or knave. The Horners also suggest that the nursery rhyme originated in a chapbook called *The History Of Jack Horner. Containing The Witty Pranks He Play'd, From His Youth To His Riper Years, Being Pleasant For Winter Evenings* (catchy title) which was printed around 1770. In fact, the chapbook contains a rather muddled version and is likely to have used the much older nursery rhyme for the already well-known name.

In the Horners' favour, there is nothing in print connecting 'Little Jack Horner' to Thomas Horner and Mells until the nineteenth century. But when Richard Whiting was arrested and put on trial, Thomas Horner was a member of the jury that condemned the abbott to be hung, drawn and quartered at Glastonbury Tor on 15 November 1539, his head fastened to the gates of his now deserted and looted abbey. A Somerset rhyme also recalls:

Hopton, Horner, Smyth, and Thynne,
When abbots went out, they came in.

Little Miss Muffet

Little Miss Muffet
Sat on a tuffet,
Eating her curds and whey;
There came a big spider,
Who sat down beside her,
And frightened Miss Muffet away.

Millais painted *Little Miss Muffet* in 1884 and this is a very popular nursery rhyme. There is speculation that it was written by Dr Thomas Moffat, a renowned entomologist and doctor from the reign of James I. He was largely responsible for *Theatrum Insectorum*, the first scientific study of insects, although it was not published until after his death in 1604. He studied silkworms in Italy and was fascinated by arthropods, particularly spiders, and as he had a daughter called Patience, the story could easily fit.

Or could the rhyme really be about Mary Queen of Scots, frightened by the strict Protestant clergyman and religious reformer, John Knox?

It has also been suggested that the idea of sitting, waiting for something important or significant to happen, is a common theme in many nursery rhymes, echoing pagan customs dating back to the Dark Ages.

In case you wondered, a tuffet can mean a tuft or clump of grass, a small mound or low seat such as a stool. The closest modern equivalent of curds and whey is probably cottage cheese.

Little Polly Flinders

> Little Polly Flinders,
> Sat among the cinders,
> Warming her pretty little toes;
> Her mother came and caught her,
> And whipped her little daughter,
> For spoiling her nice new clothes.

Like Miss Muffet, Polly Flinders is sitting, perhaps waiting, but little is known of the rhyme's origins. It was first recorded as 'Little Jenny Flinders' in *Original Ditties For The Nursery* printed around 1805. It would not have been unusual for girls, and children in general, to be physically punished and there were even specially designed 'whipping stools' for the purpose.

There are echoes of Cinderella in the rhyme but it was probably simply meant as a cautionary tale.

Little Tommy Tucker

> Little Tommy Tucker,
> Sings for his supper;
> What shall we give him?
> White bread and butter.
> How shall he cut it without a knife?
> How will he be married without a wife?

I always knew it as brown bread and butter, which would have been the cheaper, more rustic option in days gone by. 'Tommy Tucker' was sometimes used as a colloquial term for an orphan and the idea of singing for your supper was a proverbial phrase commonly used from the seventeenth century and possibly earlier; the low social status of orphans at that time would have made it difficult to find a wife.

Various Thomas Tuckers have been suggested to have inspired the rhyme: a scholar and bachelor of arts at St John's College, Oxford, who was appointed 'Prince or Lorde of the Revells' in 1607; and 'Tom Tuck', who appears in *Witt's Recreations* by John Herrick in 1640.

Lucy Locket Lost Her Pocket

> Lucy Locket lost her pocket,
> Kitty Fisher found it;
> Not a penny was there in it,
> Only ribbon round it.

This is one of those rhymes where the names are so specific it seems that it has to be about real people with a true story to tell. Halliwell, who included it in his collection of 1842, claimed it was about 'two celebrated courtesans of the time of Charles II'.

A famous eighteenth-century courtesan was also called Kitty Fisher. Born Catherine Marie Fischer, she was painted by Sir Joshua Reynolds along with several other artists, and was the subject of many songs and verses around the middle of the century. Lucy Locket is a character in Gay's *The Beggar's Opera* in 1728, but he may have been using a traditional name rather than basing her on a real person.

The rhyme was already popular in America and Britain at the beginning of the nineteenth century. It is sung to the tune of 'Yankee Doodle', which appeared in the US around the mid-eighteenth century but the tune may have been added later or changed over the years.

Mary, Mary, Quite Contrary

Mary, Mary, quite contrary,
How does your garden grow?
With silver bells and cockle shells,
And pretty maids all in a row.

Its origins are hotly debated and there are many theories with little real evidence to back them. Again, most focus on the turbulent Tudors and the religious upheaval of the times.

The Catholic Church

The rhyme has been seen as a general allegory of the Catholic Church in the sixteenth century with the bells representing the *sanctus* bells, the cockle shells the badges worn by pilgrims, and the pretty maids being the nuns. Whether it is mourning the persecution of the Catholic Church by Henry VIII and Elizabeth I, or its reinstatement under Mary Tudor, is not clear.

Mary, Mary

Traditionally, Mary is taken to be Mary Queen of Scots. 'How does your garden grow?' could refer to her reign in Scotland. With her French courtly manners and Catholicism, the vivacious Mary was seen as very frivolous by the sober religious leader John Knox, who strongly disapproved of her. The silver bells would again be the Catholic cathedral bells; the cockle shells might be the decorations on a dress given to Mary by her husband the Dauphin of France, or could suggest her second husband Robert Darnley was unfaithful to her; the pretty maids were her ladies-in-waiting, the so-called 'Four Marys'.

Another possible Mary is Mary Tudor, or Mary I of England. It is suggested that the rhyme mocks the fact that she had no children – the pretty maids referring to her miscarriages – or that during her five-year reign, England became a Catholic dependent of Spain; Mary was married to Philip II of Spain. Garden may even be a pun on the name of her chief minister, Stephen Gardiner. Mary could be regarded as 'quite contrary' because she reversed the religious changes of her father Henry VIII and brother Edward VI, and restored Roman Catholicism, earning herself the title 'Bloody Mary' through her persecution of dissenters. The 'silver bells and cockle shells' were instruments to torture the hapless Protestant martyrs: silver bells are said to be thumbscrews, and cockle shells a device attached to the genitals. The pretty maids, it is argued, stood for the 'Maiden', an early version of the guillotine, and 'all in a row' is a reference to those burned at the stake.

The earliest printed version of the nursery rhyme appeared around 1744. Others followed with slight variations in wording, particularly for the final line. One ended with 'Sing cuckolds all in a row', which is also the name of a seventeenth-century ballad.

Old Mother Goose

> Old Mother Goose,
> When she wanted to wander,
> Would ride through the air
> On a very fine gander.

The verse is taken from the beginning of the chapbook story of the goose that laid the golden egg, published at the start of the nineteenth century. This mother goose is occasionally illustrated as a real goose wearing a bonnet, or, more often, as a witch-like character, but the name itself is far more important, and has long been associated with nursery rhymes and stories.

The American Mother Goose
In the US, nursery rhymes are still known as Mother Goose rhymes, sometimes said to be named after Elizabeth Vergoose of Boston. Born Elizabeth Foster in Charlestown, Massachusetts, in 1655, she married Isaac Vergoose, raising ten stepchildren from his first marriage plus six more of

her own. Her daughter, also named Elizabeth, married Thomas Fleet, publisher of the *Boston Evening Post*, and it is suggested he published his mother-in-law's verses and stories in 1719, in a book called *Songs For The Nursery; Mother Goose's Melodies For Children*, which came to be known as Mother Goose rhymes. The problem with this story is that no copy of such a book has ever been found.

French Connections

All the evidence suggests the character originated in France. A monthly chronicle by Jean Loret appeared in 1650 containing the line 'Like a Mother Goose story', showing the idea was already familiar, and the character is mentioned in earlier French writings around 1620. Then, in 1697, Charles Perrault published a collection called *Histories Or Tales Of Long Ago With Morals*. The title page had the line '*Contes De Ma Mère L'Oye*' – 'Tales Of Mother Goose'. It included many of the folk stories we associate with Mother Goose, such as 'Cinderella' and 'Little Red Riding Hood', but none of the nursery rhymes.

English Roots

Perrault's stories were translated into English in 1729 with the same title page line, 'Tales Of Mother Goose'. Collections of children's stories and rhymes began to be printed more widely, but it was not until around 1765 that *Mother Goose's Melody – Or Sonnets For The Cradle* appeared. This was registered as a published book in 1780. It was described as containing 'the most celebrated songs and lullabies of the old British nurses' and included some verses of Shakespeare. Six years later in 1786, the first authorized edition of the book was printed in the US in Worcester, Massachusetts.

And who was Mother Goose? The most likely answer is that she was not a specific person at all and that it was simply a generic name for a countrywoman. It does emphasize the idea that rhymes and stories were traditionally told by women.

Old Mother Hubbard

Old Mother Hubbard
Went to the cupboard,
To fetch her poor dog a bone;
But when she got there,
The cupboard was bare,
And so the poor dog had none.

She went to the baker's
To buy him some bread;
But when she came back,
The poor dog was dead.

She went to the undertaker's
To buy him a coffin;
But when she came back,
The poor dog was laughing.

She took a clean dish
To get him some tripe;
But when she came back,
He was smoking a pipe.

She went to the alehouse
To get him some beer;
But when she came back,
The dog sat in a chair.

She went to the tavern
For white wine and red;
But when she came back,
The dog stood on his head.

She went to the fruiterer's
To buy him some fruit;
But when she came back,
He was playing the flute.

She went to the tailor's
To buy him a coat;
But when she came back,
He was riding a goat.

She went to the hatter's
To buy him a hat;
But when she came back,
He was feeding the cat.

She went to the barber's
To buy him a wig;
But when she came back,
He was dancing a jig.

She went to the cobbler's
To buy him some shoes;
But when she came back,
He was reading the news.

She went to the seamstress
To buy him some linen;
But when she came back,
The dog was a-spinning.

She went to the hosier's
To buy him some hose;
But when she came back,
He was dressed in his clothes.

> The dame made a curtsey,
> The dog made a bow;
> The dame said, Your servant,
> The dog said, Bow-wow.

First published as a book called *The Comic Adventures Of Old Mother Hubbard And Her Dog* in 1805, the rhyme was an instant hit. The publisher, J. Harris, claimed almost 10,000 copies were sold in just a few months. He reprinted the following year and capitalized on its success with a longer version and sequel.

The Author

Unusually, the rhyme is not anonymous. It was written by Sarah Catherine Martin in 1804, in Kitley, Devon, while staying with her sister Judith Ann Martin and her future brother-in-law, the wonderfully named John Pollexfen Bastard, MP. When it was published, readers believed it was a political satire, which possibly accounts for its popularity.

Evidence suggests the first three verses were a traditional rhyme and that Sarah Martin added eleven more, continuing the tale. A similar rhyme called 'Old Dame Trot' had been published in 1803 and there are links to the *Infant Institutes* version of 'There Was an Old Woman Who Lived in a Shoe' from 1797.

Sarah Martin is said to have been an attractive, lively and talkative young woman who enjoyed entertaining fellow guests with her stories. William IV pursued her for some time before he became king – there's no suggestion he ever caught her.

Origins of the Name

Mother Hubbard was used as a character as early as 1591, although not in anything bearing any resemblance to the nursery rhyme. It's occasionally suggested that she was based on St Hubert, the patron saint of hunters whose help was invoked to cure rabies. It has even been claimed that the older first three verses refer to Cardinal Wolsey's refusal to grant Henry VIII a divorce from Catherine of Aragon.

The Man in the Moon

The man in the moon,
Came down too soon,
And asked the way to Norwich;
He went by the south,
And burnt his mouth,
With supping cold plum porridge.

The man in the moon is a familiar figure in folklore, inspired by the 'face' that is clearly visible on a bright full moon. Many ancient myths explain how he came to be there, usually as punishment for some crime. In Norse mythology, Mani is the personification of the moon: he crosses the skies in a horse and carriage, chased by the Great Wolf, Hati, to Ragnarok. Christian traditions link him to the man found gathering sticks on the Sabbath, or to Cain the wanderer, condemned to circle the Earth for ever.

There are several versions of 'The Man in the Moon' nursery rhyme, where he drinks claret or is caught in a trap, and this particular version has an alternative last line: 'By eating cold pease-porridge.' It was well known in America and Britain by the beginning of the nineteenth century but the suggestion that the melody comes from a sixteenth-century tune may mean it is much older.

Wee Willie Winkie

Wee Willie Winkie runs through the town,
Upstairs and downstairs, in his nightgown,
Rapping at the window, crying through the lock,
Are the children in their beds, for it's now ten o'clock.

Hey, Willie Winkie, are you coming in?
The cat is singing purring sounds to the sleeping hen,
The dog's spread out on the floor, and doesn't give a
　　cheep,

But here's a wakeful little boy who will not fall asleep!

Anything but sleep, you rogue! glowering like the
    moon,
Rattling in an iron jug with an iron spoon,
Rumbling, tumbling round about, crowing like a cock,
Shrieking like I don't know what, waking sleeping folk.

Hey, Willie Winkie – the child's in a creel!
Wriggling from everyone's knee like an eel,
Tugging at the cat's ear, and confusing all her thrums,
Hey, Willie Winkie – see, there he comes!

Weary is the mother who has a dusty child,
A small short little child, who can't run on his own,
Who always has a battle with sleep before he'll close
    an eye,
But a kiss from his rosy lips gives strength anew to me.

The poem was written by
William Miller for the 1841
book, *Whistle-Binkie: Stories For
The Fireside*. Jacobite songs use
the name Wee Willie Winkie
to mean William III of Orange,
who ruled Britain with his wife,
Mary II, from 1689 until her
death in 1694, and then as sole
monarch until 1702.

Miller was probably just using the name rather than writing a political parody. As often happened, he may have started with an older traditional rhyme and added extra verses. He originally wrote the poem in Scots with English versions appearing from 1844.

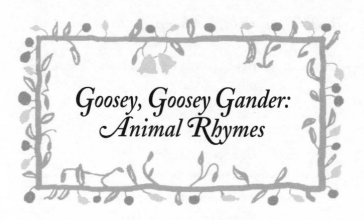

Goosey, Goosey Gander:
Animal Rhymes

There is a rich strand of folklore and superstition concerning animals and some rhymes hark back to these ancient legends. Others are slightly more recent and the same references to people, politics, and events that lie behind so many nursery rhymes in general have also inspired animal rhymes, from the thirteenth-century wool tax of 'Baa, Baa, Black Sheep' to the genuinely innocent story of a small girl and her orphaned pet lamb.

Baa, Baa, Black Sheep

Baa, Baa, Black Sheep,
Have you any wool?
Yes sir, yes sir,
Three bags full;
One for the master,
And one for the dame,
And one for the little boy,
Who lives down the lane.

There seems to be lots of talk about the origins of this rhyme but rather fewer facts. It is sung to a version of an old French tune called '*Ah! Vous Dirai-Je, Maman*', which is also used for 'Twinkle, Twinkle' and 'The Alphabet Song' from *Sesame Street*, and it was the first song to be played digitally on a computer. 'Baa, Baa, Black Sheep' was included in the earliest printed collection of nursery rhymes, *Tommy Thumb's Pretty Song Book*, around 1744, but the words and music first appeared together in *Nursery Songs And Games*, published in Philadelphia in 1879.

It is said to refer to the export tax imposed on wool in England in 1275, which remained in force until the fifteenth century and was very unpopular.

In the twentieth century, the rhyme provoked a row over its political correctness with suggestions that it had links to the slave trade. There is no evidence for this and in fact black wool was probably used because it was particularly valuable.

Barber, Barber, Shave a Pig

Barber, barber, shave a pig,
How many hairs to make a wig?
Four and twenty, that's enough,
Give the barber a pinch of snuff.

Very little is known about the history of this rhyme but it appears in nursery-rhyme collections from the beginning of the nineteenth century. It may have been an old joke on the idea that there was absolutely no profit to be made from shaving a pig.

Ding, Dong, Bell, Pussy's in the Well

Ding, dong, bell,
Pussy's in the well.
Who put her in?
Little Johnny Green.
Who pulled her out?
Little Tommy Stout.
What a naughty boy was that,
To try to drown poor pussycat,
Who never did him any harm,
And killed the mice in his father's barn.

The rhyme has a long history, the first reference to it being made in 1580 by John Lant, the organist at Winchester Cathedral. The phrase 'Ding, dong, bell' also appears in several Shakespeare plays including *The Taming Of The Shrew*, *The Tempest* and *The Merchant Of Venice*, although it has been suggested that Shakespeare simply meant to indicate sound effects.

The rhyme was first printed in something like its modern form in 1765. And there are various versions, some with the names Tommy O'Linne and Tommy Quin, which the Opies suggest come from another rhyme with the rather jokey-sounding title, 'Tom A Lin And His Wife, And His Wife's Mother'.

The earliest versions leave the poor cat to drown and the rhyme has lost popularity in recent times because of the cruelty to animals. There is even a modern, cleaned-up version where the cat is found 'at the well' rather than in it.

Goosey, Goosey Gander

> Goosey, goosey gander,
> Whither shall I wander?
> Upstairs and downstairs,
> And in my lady's chamber.
> There I met an old man
> Who would not say his prayers.
> I took him by the left leg,
> And threw him down the stairs.

A slightly different version was printed in 1784, but it is possible that the first and last four lines were originally two separate rhymes. The Opies point to a playground chant about craneflies that is very similar to the second half:

> Old father Long-legs
> Can't say his prayers:
> Take him by the left leg,
> And throw him downstairs.

Turbulent Times

There is also speculation that its historical roots lie in the religious persecutions of England's eleven-year period as a republican Commonwealth from 1649 until 1660. Catholic priests took refuge in priest's holes in some of the country's grandest houses; if caught, the priests and the families hiding them could face execution.

And the evidence? 'Goosey, goosey' could be seen as a reference to Cromwell's Roundheads marching in goose-step, and an old nickname from the period called Catholics 'left-footers'.

Others have pointed to the religious propaganda campaign waged against the Catholic Church by Henry VIII for the rhyme's origins.

Hickety, Pickety, My Black Hen

Hickety, pickety, my black hen,
She lays eggs for gentlemen;
Gentlemen come every day,
To see what my black hen doth lay.
Sometimes nine and sometimes ten,
Hickety, pickety, my black hen.

The first known publication date is 1853 but almost nothing is known of this rhyme's origins. The words sometimes vary, another Victorian version begins with 'Mittie Mattie had a hen', and many people know it as 'Higgledy piggledy', which was a term probably first used by pig farmers.

It has been pointed out by people who keep chickens that it would be a rare hen that could regularly lay nine or ten eggs for anyone.

Hickory, Dickory, Dock

Hickory, dickory, dock,
The mouse ran up the clock.
The clock struck one,
The mouse ran down,
Hickory, dickory, dock.

This is an action rhyme where children are encouraged to mimic and count out the chimes of a clock. Its earliest publication date is 1744, in *Tommy Thumb's Pretty Little Song Book*, although it is far older than that.

There are claims that it is American in origin. Hickory comes from the Native American word 'pawcohiccora' for the milky, oily liquid extracted from hickory nuts, and the pohickory was listed as one of the types of tree found growing in Virginia in 1653. Dock could refer to the widespread plant whose leaves are used to soothe nettle stings.

However, there are also suggestions that the rhyme originated in Cumbria with the Westmorland shepherds' archaic number system for counting sheep – *hevera* for eight, *devera* for nine and *dick* for ten. The numbers would obviously tie in with the idea of a clock.

The nursery rhyme also seems to have been well known in Scotland. An 1821 edition of *Blackwood's Magazine* describes children in Edinburgh frequently using the rhyme to decide who should begin a game.

Horsey, Horsey

> Horsey, horsey, don't you stop,
> Just let your feet go clipetty clop;
> Your tail goes swish and the wheels go round,
> Giddy-up! We're homeward bound.

This is a fun action rhyme for children, and useful as a simple introduction to the idea of sounds and onomatopoeia. Although it uses 'giddy-up', a traditional English term, the rhyme is modern, written in 1938 by Paddy Roberts and Ralph Butler. It was made popular by bandleaders including Henry Hall and his Orchestra on the BBC, and Billy Cotton.

I Love Little Pussy

> I love little pussy,
> Her coat is so warm,
> And if I don't hurt her
> She'll do me no harm.
> So I'll not pull her tail,
> Nor drive her away,
> But pussy and I
> Very gently will play.

This verse was published in 1829 in a catchily titled book, *Hints For The Formation Of Infant Schools, With An Account Of The Apparatus, And A Selection Of Hymns And Verses, Adapted To These Schools*. The idea of improving morality verses for children appealed to the Victorians and the rhyme quickly gained popularity on both sides of the Atlantic.

Incy Wincy Spider

> Incy Wincy Spider
> Climbed up the water spout;
> Down came the rain,
> And washed poor Incy out.
> Out came the sunshine
> Dried up all the rain,
> And Incy Wincy Spider
> Climbed up the spout again.

This is an action rhyme using the fingers to show the spider climbing, the rain falling, and the sun coming out, only for the spider to begin to climb again. It is fairly recent in comparison with other popular nursery rhymes and probably originated in America at the beginning of the twentieth century.

Ladybird, Ladybird

Ladybird, ladybird,
Fly away home,
Your house is on fire
And your children have flown.

All except one,
And that's little Ann,
And she has crept under
The frying pan.

I was always taught to recite the rhyme if a ladybird landed on me, blowing gently if it failed to fly. Some people believe that if you make a wish and the beetle flies but lands on you again, your wish will come true.

There is an old superstition that it's bad luck to kill one and the rhyme was possibly chanted by farm workers warning ladybirds to flee before they burned stubble in fields after the harvest. Ladybirds would certainly have been encouraged because they kill aphids and other pests.

Sacred Names
In the US, ladybirds are usually called ladybugs but literal translations of the name from other languages show the small beetle has always had religious associations – 'Mary's gold' in German, 'God's little cow' in Spanish and 'Insect of a good God' in French, are just a few examples. And the name ladybird comes from 'Our Lady's bird'.

Witchcraft

There was a theory that the rhyme was really a charm against witches, always useful in the Middle Ages when it was believed you could get rid of a witch by telling her that her home was ablaze. The sacred overtones to the ladybird's name and the idea that it is unlucky to kill them suggest this was never the case.

Lost in Antiquity

The rhyme is likely to be extremely old, certainly predating its first appearance in print in 1744 by centuries. The fact that very similar versions can be found in many different countries, even including the name Ann, point to origins in antiquity.

In Germany, the rhyme is said to have been a charm to guard and speed the sun as it sets; other traditional tales link ladybirds to ancient Egyptian scarabs and beliefs about Isis, or to Norse mythology and worship of the goddess of love and fertility, Freya.

Mary Had a Little Lamb

Mary had a little lamb,
Its fleece was white as snow,
And everywhere that Mary went,
The lamb was sure to go.

It followed her to school one day,
That was against the rule,
It made the children laugh and play,
To see a lamb at school.

And so the teacher turned it out,
But still it lingered near,
And waited patiently about,
Till Mary did appear.

Why does the lamb love Mary so?
The eager children cry,
Why, Mary loves the lamb, you know,
The teacher did reply.

This is an American rhyme written by Sarah Josepha Hale
of Boston, in May 1830, and is said to have been inspired
by a real incident.

Encouraged by her brother, young Mary Sawyer of
Stirling, Massachusetts, took her pet lamb to school causing
great excitement among her classmates. It is not unusual,

even today, for orphaned 'cade' lambs to be hand-reared, and they can become very attached to their adoptive parent.

You can still see Redstone School where Mary took her lamb, although it is now in Sudbury, Massachusetts, having been restored and moved there by Henry Ford. It is sometimes claimed that the first verse was not written by Sarah Hale but by John Roulstone, who happened to be visiting the school on the same day as the lamb.

'Mary had a little lamb' were the first words to be recorded by Thomas Edison on his phonograph.

Pop Goes the Weasel

Up and down the City Road,
In and out the Eagle,
That's the way the money goes,
Pop goes the weasel.

Half a pound of tuppenny rice,
Half a pound of treacle,
That's the way the money goes,
Pop goes the weasel.

The words were written around the middle of the nineteenth century for an older tune. It quickly crossed to America where it's said to have sparked a dance craze, although the lyrics vary and the US versions are quite different. It has been used for a singing game where several rings are formed and various people are appointed weasels.

Partly because there are so many variations, the words are open to interpretation. It's been suggested 'pop goes the weasel' refers to a hatter's or spinner's mechanical tool for measuring thread which made a popping sound, a tailor's heavy iron, or that it is cockney rhyming slang for coat – weasel and stoat – which was pawned or popped.

Music Halls

The Eagle is probably the Eagle pub, which stands at the corner of City Road and Shepherdess Walk in East London and has a wall plaque with the words of the nursery rhyme. An older tavern on the site was rebuilt as a music hall in 1825 by 'Bravo' Rouse. It was later demolished and rebuilt again as a public house in 1901.

In towns and cities, light entertainment acts were often staged in the back rooms of pubs, in 'song and supper' rooms particularly for men, at travelling fairs and pleasure gardens. From the early nineteenth century, these venues began to be brought together and music halls were purpose built, often by landlords behind their pubs. They kept the traditional informal, sometimes raucous, atmosphere of a tavern, with eating, drinking and smoking continuing throughout performances with audiences joining in. By the middle of the century, they were very popular and it would be easy to spend a lot of money in one. You can still see an example of a surviving pub music hall at Wilton's in East London, not far from Tower Bridge.

Six Little Mice Sat Down to Spin

Six little mice sat down to spin;
Pussy passed by and she peeped in.
What are you doing, my little men?
Weaving coats for gentlemen.
Shall I come in and cut off your threads?
No, no, Mistress Pussy, you'd bit off our heads.
Oh no, I'll not, I'll help you to spin.
That may be so, but you can't come in.

Sadly nothing seems to be known about the history of this rhyme other than it was first printed around 1840. Beatrix Potter famously had her little mice sing a version of it to mock Simpkin the cat in *The Tailor Of Gloucester*.

The Lion and the Unicorn

The lion and the unicorn
Were fighting for the crown;
The lion beat the unicorn
All round the town.

Some gave them white bread,
And some gave them brown;
Some gave them plum cake
And drummed them out of town.

Unicorns are mythical beasts and traditional rivals of lions. Both have been called the king of the beasts and they are seen as complementary – one fiery, the other cool, the lion's sun to the unicorn's moon, with neither the ultimate victor.

This rhyme is usually thought to refer to the union of England and Scotland under James I of England and VI of Scotland in 1603, on the death of Elizabeth I. This meant a new coat of arms was needed to represent Britain, combining the lion of England and the unicorn of Scotland. As the lion is shown wearing the crown, he could be said to have beaten the unicorn.

King James himself wrote of the heraldic union in terms of two formerly warring nations united in a new balanced order.

A version of the rhyme, printed in a chapbook of 1806, has a different second verse, which was probably the original:

And when he had beat him out,
He beat him in again;
He beat him three times over,
His power to maintain.

This gives a tantalizing hint that it is referring to specific battles but sadly it gives no clue as to which ones.

Gladstone and Disraeli

Lewis Carroll included the lion and the unicorn as characters in *Through The Looking Glass And What Alice Found There*, with the pair fighting for the White King's crown. Sir John Tenniel's illustrations for the book caricature the Whig Gladstone as the lion and Tory Disraeli as the unicorn, reflecting their many heated parliamentary battles.

Three Blind Mice

Three blind mice, three blind mice,
See how they run, see how they run,
They all run after the farmer's wife,
Who cut off their tails with the carving knife,
Did you ever see such a thing in your life,
As three blind mice.

For such an old rhyme, 'Three Blind Mice' has a well-documented history. It dates back to 1609 and a book of musical rounds called *Pleasant Roundelaies*, edited and perhaps written by a teenage Thomas Ravenscroft, a recent choral scholar at St Paul's. The eighteenth-century writer James Boswell mentioned it in his famous diaries, and a century later, Rimbault included the tune in one of his musical collections. It was probably not intended as a nursery song for children initially.

Suggestions that the rhyme was actually written earlier and that link it to Mary I and her persecution of three Protestant bishops seem to be unfounded. The Oxford Martyrs, Ridley, Latimer and Cranmer, were not blind and were burned at the stake rather than executed with a sword, so words and theory do not fit together.

To Market, to Market, to Buy a Fat Pig

> To market, to market, to buy a fat pig,
> Home again, home again, jiggety-jig;
> To market, to market, to buy a fat hog,
> Home again, home again, jiggety-jog.

An early version, without the pig, was included in John Florio's dictionary of 1598, *A Worlde Of Wordes*:

To market, to market,
To buy a plum bun:
Home again, home again,
Market is done.

It was also in the revised edition of 1611 and it is probable Florio knew the rhyme from his childhood. It does not appear again in print until the beginning of the nineteenth century.

Two Little Dicky Birds

Two little dicky birds sitting on a wall,
One named Peter, one named Paul;
Fly away, Peter! Fly away, Paul!
Come back, Peter! Come back, Paul!

Small squares of paper are stuck on each index finger to represent the two birds, perched on the edge of a table. They bounce up and down until first one and then the other flies away fast behind the shoulder, and instantly the index fingers are replaced with the middle fingers on the table edge minus the paper birds. The reverse happens at 'Come back' when the paper birds return.

My mother never managed to convince me that this was really magic and I can still remember the frustration of knowing there was trickery but not being able to work it out.

> **Old Tricks**
>
> The novelist Laetitia Mathilda Hawkins wrote how the eighteenth-century poet and playwright Oliver Goldsmith kept her entertained with the trick when she was a small child, and the simple sleight of hand has probably been used to amuse children for hundreds of years.

The rhyme was first printed in *Mother Goose's Melody* in 1765 when the birds' names were Jack and Jill. They were probably changed to the apostles' names Peter and Paul by the virtuous Victorians at some point in the nineteenth century.

Who Killed Cock Robin?

Who killed Cock Robin?
I, said the Sparrow,
With my bow and arrow,
I killed Cock Robin.

Who saw him die?
I, said the Fly,
With my little eye,
I saw him die.

Who caught his blood?
I, said the Fish,
With my little dish,
I caught his blood.

Who'll make the shroud?
I, said the Beetle,
With my thread and needle,
I'll make the shroud.

Who'll dig his grave?
I, said the Owl,
With my pick and shovel,
I'll dig his grave.

Who'll be the parson?
I, said the Rook,
With my little book,
I'll be the parson.

Who'll be the clerk?
I, said the Lark,
If it's not in the dark,
I'll be the clerk.

Who'll carry the link?
I, said the Linnet,
I'll fetch it in a minute,
I'll carry the link.

Who'll be chief mourner?
I, said the Dove,
I mourn for my love,
I'll be chief mourner.

Who'll carry the coffin?
I, said the Kite,
If it's not through the night,
I'll carry the coffin.

Who'll bear the pall?
We, said the Wren,
Both the cock and the hen,
We'll bear the pall.

Who'll sing the psalm?
I, said the Thrush,
As she sat on a bush,
I'll sing the psalm.

Who'll toll the bell?
I, said the Bull,
Because I can pull,
I'll toll the bell.

All the birds of the air
Fell a-sighing and a-sobbing,
When they heard the bell toll
For poor Cock Robin.

There are various ideas about the rhyme's origins ranging from historical events to legends. One of the most widely circulated is that it is a parody of the fall of Robert Walpole's government in 1742, just two years before the rhyme first appeared in print.

Older Origins
However, there are suggestions the rhyme may be older. There are similarities to the poet John Skelton's 'The Boke of Phyllyp Sparowe' written in 1508; his lament for a dead bird was in turn inspired by the Roman poet Catullus.

Buckland Rectory in Gloucestershire has also been linked to the rhyme. A fifteenth-century stained-glass window there seems to show a robin shot by an arrow, although there is some doubt whether this is a robin or a type of grouse, and several birds are shot rather than one.

William Rufus
The rhyming of 'Owl' with 'shovel' could indicate fourteenth-century Middle English and an earlier event.

William II, also known as William Rufus (the Red), was killed in 1100, in mysterious circumstances. While out hunting in the New Forest, he was shot by an arrow. A contemporary account describes him being carried home, his chest soaked with blood. The third son of William the Conqueror, he was succeeded as king by his younger brother Henry, who had also been out with the fateful hunting party.

There is a wilder theory that William Rufus was a heathen and his death was part of an ancient pagan fertility ritual in which a king was sacrificed to ensure a good harvest.

Ancient Myths and Stories

There are also versions of the poem in several other countries, which could mean its roots lie in a shared mythology. The story of the Norse god Balder, who was shot by arrows, is one suggestion.

More recently it has been linked to the English folklore hero Robin Hood, but this seems to be largely because of the name.

Birds and Bulls

I was always curious about the sudden appearance of a huge bull among all the other birds. This is probably a modern misinterpretation with 'bull' a shortened form of bullfinch rather than meaning the large mammal.

Oranges and Lemons: Songs and Games

Nursery rhymes such as 'Lavender's Blue' were adapted from older folk songs; others first appeared in songbooks from the seventeenth century onwards, with words set to music, several sharing the same tunes. The fact they were sung made them popular for children's games. In both 'London Bridge' and 'Oranges and Lemons', players choose sides and it is hard to ignore the chilling echoes of pre-Christian rituals.

Bobby Shafto

> Bobby Shafto's gone to sea,
> Silver buckles at his knee;
> He'll come back and marry me,
> Bonny Bobby Shafto.

> Bobby Shafto's bright and fair,
> Combing down his yellow hair;
> He's my love for evermore,
> Bonny Bobby Shafto.
>
> Bobby Shafto's looking out,
> All his ribbons flew about,
> All the ladies gave a shout,
> Hey for Bobby Shafto!

The Shafto family take their name from the village of Shaftoe in Northumberland and their family estate is in Whitworth, near Spennymoor, County Durham. There have been a number of Robert Shaftos over the years but the nursery rhyme is probably about the handsome 'Bonnie Bobby' Shafto who became Tory MP for County Durham from 1760 to 1768. The family may have owned ships and the song is said to have been used to support Bobby's election campaign.

Bonnie Bobby

He was born in 1732 and there is a portrait showing him as a young man with blond hair, possibly by Sir Joshua Reynolds. He was quite the charmer and very popular with women, who although they were not allowed to vote, may have influenced their husbands in his favour.

He is said to have broken many hearts including that of Miss Bellasyse of Brancepeth Castle, reputed to have died for love in 1774, although it may have been tuberculosis. The same year, Bonnie Bobby married another heiress, Anne Duncombe of Duncombe Park in Yorkshire. She inherited property in Downton in Wiltshire, where Bobby Shafto became Whig MP in 1780 having switched political allegiance to support William Pitt the Younger.

He died in 1797 and is buried in the Shafto family crypt in Whitworth Church.

Boys and Girls Come Out to Play

Boys and girls come out to play,
The moon doth shine as bright as day.
Leave your supper and leave your sleep,
And join your playfellows in the street.
Come with a whoop and come with a call,
Come with a good will or not at all.
Up the ladder and down the wall,
A halfpenny loaf will serve us all.
You find milk and I'll find flour,
And we'll have a pudding in half an hour.

Maybe I've seen too many chilling films with eerie versions featured on the soundtrack but this rhyme has always seemed slightly sinister to me.

I remember it as a playground skipping game but it has a long history. Probably dating from the mid-seventeenth century, it is first recorded in adult dance books from 1708 and, more surprisingly, quoted in political satires. It seems to have quickly become widely known; Samuel Johnson wrote, 'Come with a whoop and come with a call, Come with a good will or not at all', in a letter to Mrs Thrale encouraging her to return home from Brighton in 1778.

By the end of Queen Anne's reign in 1714, the rhyme was already associated with children. It was popular from America to the South of France as a children's call to evening games, presumably in the summer after the heat of the day, or dating from a time when most children had to work and evenings would be their only free time.

Cock a Doodle Doo

> Cock a doodle doo!
> My dame has lost her shoe,
> My master's lost his fiddling stick,
> And doesn't know what to do.

In Tudor times, mocking the cocks by chanting, 'Cock a doodle doo, Peggy hath lost her shoe', was a common game

among children and there is a shockingly gruesome story connected to the rhyme.

Dark Deeds

During the reign of Elizabeth I, a wealthy farmer called Anthony James and his wife Elizabeth were murdered by thieves who broke into their home while the servants were out at a passing fair.

Their children were then kidnapped and left at an inn in Bishop's Hatfield, Hertfordshire, where the innkeeper's wife, Annis Dell, and her son George were paid to get rid of them. The three-year-old boy, Anthony, was killed in front of his four-year-old sister Besse, whose tongue was cut out to stop her speaking about the crime. Quite what happened next to the terrified child is not known, but Anthony's body was dumped in a pond where he was found some weeks later. He was identified by his red hair and fine coat as the boy who had stayed at the Dells' inn; Annis and George Dell were arrested on suspicion of murder.

Justice

Some three years later, Besse reappeared alone at Bishop's Hatfield and was recognized as the murdered boy's sister. She was placed in the care of a kind foster mother and after a few months was out with other children in King's Park, Hatfield. They were playing 'Cock a doodle doo' when to everyone's amazement, Besse joined in. After this she began to speak freely and told the terrible tale of her brother's murder.

Besse was taken before the Justice, Sir Henry Butler, and it is recorded that the jury looked into her mouth and saw nothing but a cavity. After cross-examination her evidence was believed, and Annis and George Dell were found guilty and executed.

This came to be called the Hertfordshire miracle, although medical records of the time suggest that it was not unknown for tongueless people to recover the power of speech, especially if the tongue had not been removed professionally!

The fate of the original thieves and murderers is not known, nor whether Besse ever returned to her old home.

Here We Go Gathering Nuts in May

Here we go gathering nuts in May,
Nuts in May, nuts in May,
Here we go gathering nuts in May,
On a cold and frosty morning.

Who will you have for nuts in May,
Nuts in May, nuts in May,
Who will you have for nuts in May,
On a cold and frosty morning.

We'll have [add name] for nuts in May,
Nuts in May, nuts in May,
We'll have [name] for nuts in May,
On a cold and frosty morning.

Who will you have to fetch him [or her] away,
Fetch him away, fetch him away,
Who will you have to fetch him away,
On a cold and frosty morning.

We'll have [add name] to fetch him away,
Fetch him away, fetch him away,
We'll have [name] to fetch him away,
On a cold and frosty morning.

It used to be sung as a game pairing boys and girls. Alice Gomme included the rhyme in *Traditional Games of England, Scotland, and Ireland* at the end of the nineteenth century.

Nuts could refer to ground nuts, or pig nuts, which appear in May and were typically picked by children as they grow low down and are not very plentiful. Or the line might have originally been 'knots' of May, meaning hawthorn or May blossom.

The rhyme is very similar to the older 'Here We Go Round the Mulberry Bush'.

Here We Go Round the Mulberry Bush

> Here we go round the mulberry bush,
> The mulberry bush, the mulberry bush,
> Here we go round the mulberry bush,
> On a cold and frosty morning.

This was first recorded by the Victorian collector of nursery rhymes, James Orchard Halliwell, in 1842.

Mulberries grow on trees rather than bushes and it may have started out as a bramble, or blackberry, bush. Similar rhymes are found throughout Scandinavia and the Netherlands.

The historian R. S. Duncan claimed the rhyme was about women prisoners in Wakefield prison where a mulberry tree used to grow in the exercise yard, but there is no firm evidence to support this idea.

Hey Diddle Diddle, the Cat and the Fiddle

Hey diddle diddle,
The cat and the fiddle,
The cow jumped over the moon;
The little dog laughed
To see such sport,
And the dish ran away with the spoon.

'Hey diddle diddle' is an archaic colloquial phrase used in traditional folk ballads and by Shakespeare along with other sixteenth-century writers. The rhyme was first published in 1765 in *Mother Goose's Melody* and was most likely not meant as anything other than a nonsense verse. But that hasn't stopped people speculating wildly about its origins.

Cat and Fiddle

The words 'cat and fiddle' have been said to come from Catherine of Aragon, sometimes known as Catherine la Fidèle, or from Caton le Fidèle, a supposed governor of Calais during its period of English rule from 1347 until 1558. The cat has also been identified alternately as Catherine, wife of Peter the Great, and as Sir William Catesby, speaker of the House of Commons, who opposed Richard III becoming king.

Moons and Heys

Prior Richard Moon escaped with his life after the dissolution of Bolton Abbey in 1539, but forfeited his lands and property. The Moon family had traditionally been sheep farmers and held a long-running rivalry with the Heys, another prominent Yorkshire family of cattle farmers. The Heys became Protestants just in time to escape persecution and were rewarded with much of the Moons' land and wealth.

There is a possibly apocryphal story that, defying the bitter enmity between their families, a son from one family and daughter from the other eloped in true Romeo and Juliet style.

Theories and Hoaxes

Others argue that the rhyme is an allegory for the upheavals of Tudor England representing Elizabeth I, Lady Katherine Grey and the Earls of Hertford and Leicester. Or maybe it is anti-papist, referring to Catholic priests encouraging labourers and the poor to work harder.

Halliwell supported a theory that it came from Ancient Greece, although he was probably always aware that this was a hoax.

Less earthbound ideas connect the rhyme to the constellations of Taurus, *Canis minor*, and the Big Dipper. And there are even religious theories that it describes the flight from Egypt led by Moses, or that it was connected to the Ancient Egyptians' worship of the cow goddess Hathor.

Lavender's Blue

Lavender's blue, dilly dilly, lavender's green,
When I am king, dilly, dilly, you shall be queen.
Who told you so, dilly, dilly, who told you so?
'Twas my own heart, dilly, dilly, that told me so.
Call up your men, dilly, dilly, set them to work,
Some to the plow, dilly, dilly, some to the fork,
Some to make hay, dilly, dilly, some to thresh corn,
While you and I, dilly, dilly, keep ourselves warm.

Lavender's green, dilly, dilly, lavender's blue,
If you love me, dilly, dilly, I will love you.
Let the birds sing, dilly, dilly, and the lambs play;
We shall be safe, dilly, dilly, out of harm's way.
I love to dance, dilly, dilly, I love to sing;
When I am queen, dilly, dilly, you'll be my king.
Who told me so, dilly, dilly, who told me so?
I told myself, dilly, dilly, I told me so.

There are a confusing number of versions of this song
but this is probably the best known of the more modern
ones.

It first appeared between 1672 and 1685 in a 'broadside'
or broadsheet. This original was called 'Diddle, Diddle, Or
The Kind Country Lovers'. Readers were told to sing it to
the tune of 'Lavender's Green', suggesting this was an older,
already widely known melody.

'Diddle, diddle' was a fairly bawdy song centred on drinking and sex; the narrator encourages a young woman to lie with him and 'keep the bed warm' but also seems to be asking her to love his dog as well as him:

Lavender's green, diddle diddle,
Lavender's blue
You must love me, diddle diddle,
'Cause I love you,
I heard one say, diddle diddle,
Since I came hither,
That you and I, diddle diddle,
Must lie together.

My hostess maid, diddle diddle,
Her name was Nell,
She was a lass, diddle diddle,
That I loved well,
But if she die, diddle diddle,
By some mishap,
Then she shall lie, diddle diddle,
Under the tap.

That she may drink, diddle diddle,
When she's a-dry,
Because she lov'd, diddle diddle,
My dog and I,
Call up your maids, diddle diddle,
Set them to work,

Some to make hay, diddle diddle,
Some to the rock.

Some to make hay, diddle diddle,
Some to the corn,
Whilst you and I, diddle diddle,
Keep the bed warm.
Let the birds sing, diddle diddle,
And the lambs play,
We shall be safe, diddle diddle,
Out of harm's way.

By the nineteenth century the rhyme had been cleaned up and was very much a children's nursery rhyme. It was revived in the mid-twentieth century when Burl Ives recorded a version for the film *So Dear To My Heart*, which won him an Academy Award nomination. After this, it was covered by several different singers and became a popular dance song for a time.

London Bridge is Falling Down

London Bridge is falling down,
Falling down, falling down,
London Bridge is falling down,
My fair lady.

Build it up with wood and clay,
Wood and clay, wood and clay,
Build it up with wood and clay,
My fair lady.

Wood and clay will wash away,
Wash away, wash away,
Wood and clay will wash away,
My fair lady.

Build it up with bricks and mortar,
Bricks and mortar, bricks and mortar,
Build it up with bricks and mortar,
My fair lady.

Bricks and mortar will not stay,
Will not stay, will not stay,
Bricks and mortar will not stay,
My fair lady.

Build it up with iron and steel,
Iron and steel, iron and steel,
Build it up with iron and steel,
My fair lady.

Iron and steel will bend and bow,
Bend and bow, bend and bow,
Iron and steel will bend and bow,
My fair lady.

Build it up with silver and gold,
Silver and gold, silver and gold,
Build it up with silver and gold,
My fair lady.

Silver and gold will be stolen away,
Stolen away, stolen away,
Silver and gold will be stolen away,
My fair lady.

Set a man to watch all night,
Watch all night, watch all night,
Set a man to watch all night,
My fair lady.

Suppose the man should fall asleep,
Fall asleep, fall asleep,
Suppose the man should fall asleep,
My fair lady.

Give him a pipe to smoke all night,
Smoke all night, smoke all night,
Give him a pipe to smoke all night,
My fair lady.

The first verse in particular is very well known and the rhyme has a long history. The earliest version appeared around 1744 when the first line was 'London Bridge is broken down'.

There are a number of theories about the rhyme's origins. The simplest is that it reflects the difficulty of building a bridge over the Thames and there have been several different London Bridges over the centuries.

London's Bridges

The first bridge was probably constructed as a simple military pontoon by the Romans and a wooden bridge is said to have been destroyed by Viking raiders in the eleventh century, although this is far from certain.

The first stone bridge was designed by Peter de Colechurch, a French monk, and begun in 1176. It took over thirty years to build and had twenty arches. It was something of a marvel; houses and shops were built on the bridge and it was popular with traders, possibly explaining the reference to gold and silver. There were water wheels beneath its arches for grinding grain. Over the years various arches collapsed and were rebuilt, and the Northern Gate was replaced in the sixteenth century.

By the 1820s a new bridge was needed. The twelfth-century one had survived the Great Fire of London but was showing its age and beginning to sink. The new bridge, designed by the engineer John Rennie, opened in 1831 with five stone arches.

In 1967, London Bridge was sold to Robert McCulloch of McCulloch Oil and reconstructed in Lake Havasu City in Arizona. The popular story that he thought he was buying the more interesting medieval bridge has always been denied.

The current London Bridge was designed by the architect Lord Holford and opened in 1973.

Human Sacrifice

So far the story seems quite simple but versions of the rhyme are known across Europe dating back to the fourteenth century at least. There is also a game associated with it where two players form a bridge while everyone else passes underneath holding onto the person in front, hoping not to be the one caught when the bridge falls.

This could mean that the rhyme adopted London Bridge at a later date as the most famous bridge in England and that its origins lie further back in antiquity. The mention of a watchman also echoes superstitions that malevolent water spirits must be appeased for a bridge to stand firm, hence ancient rites where people, often children, were walled into foundations to act as guardian spirits – sometimes when still alive.

Reassuringly, there is no archaeological evidence of any human remains in the foundations of London Bridge.

Lady Lea

The 1744 version of the rhyme in *Tommy Thumb's Pretty Song Book* included Lady Lea instead of 'my fair lady'. She has been identified as: Matilda of Scotland, who was married to Henry I and built a number of bridges over the river Lea, a tributary of the Thames; Henry III's wife Eleanor of Provence, who was custodian of London Bridge from 1269; and finally, a member of the Leigh family of Stoneleigh Park in Warwickshire.

London's Burning

London's burning, London's burning.
Fetch the engines, fetch the engines.
Fire! Fire! Fire! Fire!
Pour on water, pour on water.

This is a popular rhyme, usually sung as a round. Most people know that it refers to the Great Fire of London, which raged for three days in 1666, destroying a vast area of the medieval city including St Paul's Cathedral.

The Fire of London

The fire started in Pudding Lane and the narrow streets of largely wooden houses burned easily. Samuel Pepys famously described the blaze in his diary. There were surprisingly few casualties, although this may be because deaths among the poorer classes were simply not recorded. However, thousands were left homeless and many were settled elsewhere as Charles II feared rebellion. An unexpected benefit was that the fire effectively ended the plague, which had ravaged the population since 1664.

Afterwards there were many radical proposals for a modern new city designed by architects including Sir Christopher Wren but in the end, London was effectively rebuilt on the old street plan.

Fetch the Engines

It is not known exactly when the nursery rhyme was written. Contrary to popular opinion, fire engines did exist in the seventeenth century although the usual fire-fighting tool was to create a firebreak by demolishing buildings in its path. It is thought that the Great Fire was able to take such a hold on London because the mayor, Sir Thomas Bloodworth, panicked and delayed giving the order for demolition.

Oh Dear, What Can the Matter Be?

Oh dear, what can the matter be?
Dear, dear, what can the matter be?
Oh dear, what can the matter be?
Johnny's so long at the fair.

He promised he'd buy me a fairing should please me,
And then for a kiss, oh he vowed he would tease me,
He promised he'd bring me a bunch of blue ribbons
To tie up my bonny brown hair.

And it's oh dear, what can the matter be?
Dear, dear, what can the matter be?
Oh dear, what can the matter be?
Johnny's so long at the fair.

He promised to buy me a pair of sleeve buttons,
A pair of new garters that cost him but two pence,
He promised he'd bring me a bunch of blue ribbons
To tie up my bonny brown hair.

And it's oh dear, what can the matter be?
Dear, dear, what can the matter be?
Oh dear, what can the matter be?
Johnny's so long at the fair.

He promised he'd bring me a basket of posies,
A garland of lilies, a garland of roses,
A little straw hat, to set off the blue ribbons
That tie up my bonny brown hair.

The song first appeared in print as sheet music in 1792, although it is very similar to a slightly earlier Scots song. It was included in anthologies of nursery rhymes on both sides of the Atlantic from the early nineteenth century.

It immediately became very popular sung as a duet and performed in concerts. Since its first appearance it has often been parodied, from versions that mockingly commemorate George IV's coronation and the Crimean War, to the American 'Seven Old Ladies Locked in the Lavatory'.

Oh Where, Oh Where Has My Little Dog Gone?

> Oh where, oh where has my little dog gone?
> Oh where, oh where can he be?
> With his ears cut short and his tail cut long,
> Oh where, oh where can he be?

This was written by Septimus Winner, an American music publisher and critic who composed over 2,000 pieces. He registered it as a comic ballad in Philadelphia in 1864, intending it for music halls rather than children. It was originally called 'Der Deitcher's Dog' and had a further three verses telling the story of German Der Deitcher who had lost his pet dog.

The song became very popular in Britain as well as America at the turn of the century, when it was mistakenly called 'The Dutchman's Dog'.

Oranges and Lemons

Oranges and lemons,
Say the bells of St Clement's.

You owe me five farthings,
Say the bells of St Martin's.

When will you pay me?
Say the bells of Old Bailey.

When I grow rich,
Say the bells of Shoreditch.

When will that be?
Say the bells of Stepney.

I'm sure I don't know,
Says the great bell of Bow.

Here comes a candle to light you to bed,
Here comes a chopper to chop off your head.
Chip, chop, chip, chop, the last man's dead.

The game associated with the rhyme is virtually the same as the one played for 'London Bridge is Falling Down'. The two players forming the arch decide in secret which one of them is orange and which lemon, then, when the chopper falls, the person caught chooses one or other, again in secret, and then stands behind the player he finds he has chosen. The game then resumes. Towards the end of the rhyme children tend to run as fast as they can to avoid capture. When the last person has chosen sides, there is a tug of war between the two teams to decide whether oranges or lemons are the winners.

The last three lines are not included in the earliest printed version of the rhyme, which appeared around 1744, but they were perhaps added by children, as church bells were rung to mark public executions that took place at Tyburn (now Marble Arch) until 1783, when the gallows were moved to the front of Newgate prison. Executions remained public affairs until 1868, when the gallows were moved inside the prison, and they were very popular, drawing big crowds.

London's Churches and Prisons

The bells in the rhyme belong to old London churches, all within or just outside the original city walls. There is some debate about exactly which churches.

St Clement's may refer to St Clement's, Eastcheap (now Cannon Street), which is close to London Bridge and the wharves where citrus fruits would have been unloaded, although there are several other churches that are arguably closer to the Thames and docks. The other possibility is St Clement Danes near to the Courts of Justice on the Strand. A church has stood on the site for over a thousand years and tenant lawyers at St Clement's Inn within the parish were said to receive a toll for allowing oranges and lemons to be carried through to Clare Market (although that was a large meat market). A special service is held in the church each year at which the bells play 'Oranges and Lemons'.

There are also two contenders for St Martin's. One is St Martin's, Ludgate, close to St Paul's, or the more likely is St Martin Orgar on St Martin's Lane, just off Eastcheap, or Cannon Street, where moneylenders used to live and work.

Old Bailey would have been the bells of St Sepulchre, which was almost opposite the Central Criminal Court. Traditionally, the great bell of the church was rung to mark executions at Newgate Prison, next door to the Old Bailey. (The prison was demolished at the end of the nineteenth century to make way for a larger court building across both sites.) The clerk at St Sepulchre also rang a handbell outside a condemned man's cell at midnight before his execution, perhaps by candlelight. Known as the Execution Bell, it can still be viewed in the church. Incidentally, the Old Bailey was named after the street on which it stands, which follows the line of the original 'bailey' or old city wall. Fleet Prison, which was mainly used for debtors and bankrupts, was also not far away.

Shoreditch refers to St Leonard's, which is often called Shoreditch Church. It stands on the site of a Saxon church and is just outside the original city walls. It had twelve bells.

Stepney is St Dunstan's, another ancient church site just outside the city walls. It had ten bells.

St Mary-le-Bow in Cheapside was home to the great bell of Bow. According to tradition, a true cockney must be born within the sound of Bow bells.

A longer version of the rhyme also exists which includes more churches and mentions old trades and guilds in different areas of London.

Tall Tales

Apart from the obvious link to debtors and public executions, various other theories have been put forward to explain the rhyme. The execution theme and similarities to 'London Bridge' have been taken to suggest the same gruesome rituals may lie behind the two. It's even been said the words refer to Henry VIII's marriages and the untimely deaths of three of his wives. A traditional square dance called 'Oranges and Lemons' existed a century earlier but it is not known if it relates to the nursery rhyme in any way.

There are also similar rhymes linked to church bells in other parts of the country – one in Derby is recited on Shrove Tuesday at the start of a traditional football game played in the city streets. However, as church bells played such an important role throughout the ages, rung to mark events and indicate good or bad news, this is not surprising, and words were often set to bell chimes.

Polly Put the Kettle On

> Polly put the kettle on,
> Polly put the kettle on,
> Polly put the kettle on,
> We'll all have tea.
>
> Sukey take it off again,
> Sukey take it off again,
> Sukey take it off again,
> They've all gone away.

Set to an old dance tune called 'Jenny's Bawbee', the rhyme was probably written around the beginning of the nineteenth century and it was originally Molly who put the kettle on.

There have been various versions and extra verses which often included 'a drop of gin', reflecting the song's popularity as a music-hall number. It seems to have been Charles Dickens who changed the name to Polly in his reference to the rhyme in *Barnaby Rudge* in 1841.

Ride a Cock Horse to Banbury Cross

> Ride a cock horse to Banbury Cross,
> To see a fine lady upon a white horse;
> With rings on her fingers and bells on her toes,
> She shall have music wherever she goes.

There have been several rhymes about riding cock horses to various crosses from Shrewsbury to Coventry to Charing Cross, and linked to different stories, including Lady Godiva at Coventry. This is the best known and was recorded in the 1780s. Earlier versions have different descriptions of the lady – she is sometimes old, wearing a straw bonnet or riding a black horse.

It has been argued that the rhyme is older than the eighteenth century. The original Banbury Cross was destroyed around 1600 and the bells on her toes may be a reference to fifteenth-century shoes, which had bells on the pointed toes.

Horses and Fair Ladies

A cock horse is a lively, well-bred stallion but it can also mean the extra horse attached to help pull carriages uphill which were often beribboned and decorated with rosettes. Banbury Cross stood on top of a hill and it has been suggested that the fair lady was Elizabeth I, who was forced to ride the cock horse to visit the cross when her carriage lost a wheel.

Or might the fair lady have been Celia Fiennes of Broughton Castle, Banbury? She was known to have ridden throughout England on a series of journeys from 1697. It is easy to see how the original line could have been, 'To see a Fiennes lady'. However, her descendants dismiss this as an old family joke.

From the mid-sixteenth century, a cock horse could also mean a toy hobby horse, or even an adult's knee, used to bounce a young child up and down.

Ring-a-Ring o' Roses

Ring-a-ring o' roses,
A pocket full of posies,
Atishoo! Atishoo!
We all fall down.

The cows are in the meadow,
Lying fast asleep,
Atishoo! Atishoo!
We all get up.

There must have been more speculation about the meaning behind this nursery rhyme than almost any other; sadly the reality doesn't live up to the hype.

The version we know is relatively recent and not found in any anthologies before 1881. There is a record of a similar rhyme, sung to the same tune, known in Massachusetts around 1790:

Ring a ring a rosie,
A bottle full of posie,
All the girls in our town,
Ring for little Josie.

The vital 'atishoo' is missing from that and all the other earlier versions. The sneeze has been seen as the fatal last symptom of the Great Plague of 1664; 'ring-a-ring o' roses' was the rosy red rash that appeared on a victim's skin; and 'posies' of herbs would have been carried for protection. 'We all fall down' as death surely followed infection. However, this theory ignores the second verse where everyone gets up again, and also the small fact that these symptoms do not match those of the plague.

Similar rhymes, again no older than the nineteenth century, are known throughout Europe and they all suggest that the fall was meant to be a curtsey or dance movement.

Sing a Song of Sixpence

Sing a song of sixpence,
A pocket full of rye;
Four and twenty blackbirds,
Baked in a pie.

When the pie was opened,
The birds began to sing;
Was not that a dainty dish,
To set before the king?

The king was in his counting house,
Counting out his money;
The queen was in the parlour,
Eating bread and honey.

The maid was in the garden,
Hanging out the clothes,
Along came a blackbird,
And pecked off her nose.

This was said to have been written by George Steevens as a pun on Henry James Pye's unimpressive first poem as Poet Laureate in 1790, but a version had already appeared years earlier in *Tommy Thumb's Pretty Song Book* in 1744.

The rhyme may date back to the sixteenth century when it was not unusual to bake surprises into pies (Jack Horner's estate deeds are just one example). An early Italian cookery book from 1549 contains a recipe for a pie containing live birds, and chef Heston Blumenthal recreated this using twenty-four homing pigeons (blackbirds are protected) for his TV programme *Heston's Medieval Feast*.

'Counting house' also suggests sixteenth-century origins and the 'pocket full of rye' could be a reference to a specific measure from the time.

Henry VIII and All That

There are also some more far-fetched interpretations. It has been suggested that the rhyme's roots lie in folklore, so the twenty-four birds are the hours of the day, the king is the sun, the queen the moon and the blackbird is the devil stealing the maid's soul.

Like many other nursery rhymes it has been linked to Henry VIII and the dissolution of the monasteries, the blackbirds being the monks and the maid Anne Boleyn.

It has even been seen as a celebration of the King James Bible where the printed letters are the blackbirds, set up in pica form on the press. Much has also been made of apparent references to the rhyme in Shakespeare's *Twelfth*

Night and, dating from the same period, Beaumont and Fletcher's *Bonduca*.

They are interesting ideas but not backed up by any evidence.

Tom, Tom, the Piper's Son

> Tom, Tom, the piper's son,
> Stole a pig and away he run;
> The pig was eat
> And Tom was beat,
> And Tom went howling down the street.

Taken from eighteenth-century chapbooks, the rhyme probably refers to a sweet paste made with currants, commonly sold by street vendors of the time. It is often linked to a longer rhyme, which begins:

> Tom, he was a piper's son,
> He learnt to play when he was young,
> And all the tune that he could play
> Was, 'Over the hills and far away';
> Over the hills and a great way off,
> The wind shall blow my top knot off.

Both appeared in chapbooks called 'Tom The Piper's Son' around 1795, in London. This second rhyme was an adaptation of an older one sometimes associated with the Jacobites.

The phrase, 'Over the hills and far away', was already known and had been used by various writers for centuries. The tune of the same name is a traditional English folk song.

Twinkle, Twinkle, Little Star

Twinkle, twinkle, little star,
How I wonder what you are!
Up above the world so high,
Like a diamond in the sky.

When the blazing sun is gone,
When he nothing shines upon,
Then you show your little light,
Twinkle, twinkle, all the night.

Then the traveller in the dark,
Thanks you for your tiny spark,
He could not see which way to go,
If you did not twinkle so.

In the dark blue sky you keep,
And often through my curtains peep,
For you never shut your eye,
Till the sun is in the sky.

As your bright and tiny spark,
Lights the traveller in the dark,
Though I know not what you are,
Twinkle, twinkle, little star.

Most children only know the first verse, but it is from a longer poem called 'The Star' by Jane Taylor; it appeared in *Rhymes For The Nursery*, written with her sister Ann, which was first published in 1806.

The nursery rhyme is sung to the older eighteenth-century French tune '*Ah! Vous Dirai-Je, Maman*' which is also used for 'Baa, Baa, Black Sheep'. The Mad Hatter's 'Twinkle, Twinkle, Little Bat' from *Alice In Wonderland* is a well-known parody of the verse.

What Are Little Boys Made of?

What are little boys made of?
What are little boys made of?
Frogs and snails and puppy dogs' tails,
That's what little boys are made of.

What are little girls made of?
What are little girls made of?
Sugar and spice and all things nice,
That's what little girls are made of.

Robert Southey, the nineteenth-century poet, added another ten verses to these first two traditional ones. He included young men, old and young women, soldiers and sailors, as well as some proverbs, calling it 'What All The World Is Made Of'.

Yankee Doodle

Yankee Doodle came to town,
Riding on a pony;
He stuck a feather in his cap
And called it macaroni.

Chorus
Yankee Doodle keep it up,
Yankee Doodle dandy;
Mind the music and the step,
And with the girls be handy.

Father and I went down to camp,
Along with Cap'n Gooding,
And there we saw the men and boys
As thick as hasty pudding.

Chorus

And there we saw a thousand men
As rich as Squire David,
And what they wasted every day,
I wish it could be saved.

Chorus

The lasses they eat it every day,
Would keep a house a-winter,
They have so much, that I'll be bound,
They eat it when they've mind ter.

Chorus

And there I see a swamping gun,
Large as a log of maple,
Upon a deuced little cart,
A load for father's cattle.

Chorus

And every time they shoot it off,
It takes a horn of powder,
And makes a noise like father's gun,
Only a nation louder.

Chorus

I went as nigh to one myself,
As 'Siah's underpinning,
And father went as nigh again,
I thought the deuce was in him.

Chorus

Cousin Simon grew so bold,
I thought he would have cocked it,
It scared me so I shrinked it off,
And hung by father's pocket.

Chorus

And Cap'n Davis had a gun,
He kind of clapt his hand on't,
And stuck a crooked stabbing iron
Upon the little end on't.

Chorus

And there I see a pumpkin shell,
As big as mother's basin,
And every time they touched it off,
They scampered like the nation.

Chorus

I see a little barrel, too,
The heads were made of leather,
They knocked on it with little clubs,
And called the folks together.

Chorus

And there was Cap'n Washington,
And gentle folks about him,
They say he's grown so 'tarnal proud,
He will not ride without 'em.

Chorus

He got him on his meeting clothes,
Upon a slapping stallion,
He sat the world along in rows,
In hundreds and in millions.

Chorus

The flaming ribbons in his hat,
They looked so tearing fine, ah,
I wanted dreadfully to get
To give to my Jemima.

Chorus

I see another snarl of men,
A-digging graves they told me,
So 'tarnal long, so 'tarnal deep,
They 'tended they should hold me.

Chorus

It scared me so, I hooked it off,
Nor stopped, as I remember,
Nor turned about till I got home,
Locked up in mother's chamber.

Chorus

There are conflicting stories about the song's beginnings but
it definitely originated in America. For a long time parts

of it were thought to have been written by Dr Richard Shuckburgh, a British army surgeon, but this is doubtful.

At the beginning of the American War of Independence, it was sung by British troops to mock the American army's dishevelled appearance. A 'macaroni' was an eighteenth-century term for a young dandy who had taken the Grand Tour and wore very elaborate wigs, dressing in the European style. The inference was that the best the unsophisticated Americans could manage was a feather.

An early version has a verse ending, 'We will tar and feather him, And so we will John Hancock', referring to the American Revolutionary leader who became the first person to sign the Declaration of Independence in 1776. It was probably originally written about Thomas Ditson of Billerica, Massachusetts, who had been tarred and feathered for trying to buy a musket. This is why the town of Billerica is still associated with Yankee Doodle.

After the defeat of the British troops at Bunker Hill in 1775 and the battle of Lexington and Concord, the American soldiers took over the song, adapting the words to make it their own. They sang it to celebrate their victories, turning it against the British who liked it a lot less once it was used to taunt them. It has remained popular in America ever since and is Connecticut's state song.

The tune may have been taken from a Scottish air or written as a melody without words; there's also some suggestion that 'doodle' may have been a way of singing. The nursery rhyme 'Lucy Locket' is sung to the same tune.

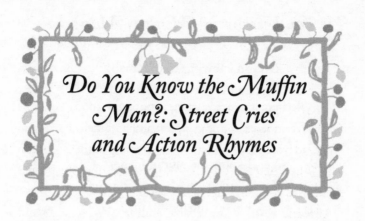

Do You Know the Muffin Man?: Street Cries and Action Rhymes

Travelling pedlars were a welcome sight in rural areas from Roman times; craftsmen, too, travelled from place to place offering their skills. There were also travelling fairs and regular markets where goods and services were bought or exchanged.

From the Middle Ages, London became a centre for sellers hoping to make their fortune in the bustling city. Everything from fruit, cakes, pies and lavender to live rabbits would be on offer. Sellers would walk the squares and streets, and to advertise their goods they would call out. They were often competing with other vendors and so their cries became increasingly inventive and musical.

Children have kept these rhymes alive, setting clapping and other games and actions to them.

Do You Know the Muffin Man?

Do you know the muffin man,
The muffin man, the muffin man,
Do you know the muffin man,
That lives in Drury Lane?

Yes, I know the muffin man,
The muffin man, the muffin man,
Yes, I know the muffin man,
Who lives in Drury Lane.

'Do You Know the Muffin Man' was first recorded around 1820 when freshly baked muffins would have been sold door to door. The rhyme refers to English muffins rather than the sweeter, cupcake-shaped American variety.

Now usually associated with theatres, in the eighteenth and early nineteenth centuries Drury Lane was one of the worst slums in London, home to gin palaces and prostitutes. There are some regional variations of the rhyme using other street names. The rhyme spread to other countries in Europe and was popular in the US from the mid-nineteenth century. Various games including forfeits, guessing and dancing have been played to the rhyme.

Hot Cross Buns

> Hot cross buns, hot cross buns,
> One a penny, two a penny,
> Hot cross buns!
> If your daughters do not like them,
> Give them to your sons;
> One a penny, two a penny,
> Hot cross buns!

This extra couplet was sometimes added:

> If you have none of these pretty little elves,
> Then you can do no better than to eat them yourselves.

This is an old street cry dating back at least to the beginning of the eighteenth century. Children would traditionally sing it on Good Friday when they ate hot cross buns for breakfast. It is sometimes linked to the child's hand game where hands are placed palm down on top of each other and the bottom one is whisked out and placed on top.

Pease Pudding Hot

Pease pudding hot,
Pease pudding cold,
Pease pudding in the pot,
Nine days old.

Some like it hot,
Some like it cold,
Some like it in the pot,
Nine days old.

The children's rhyme grew out of the food-sellers' cry announcing, 'Pease pudding hot!' often heard at fairs. It was first printed in *Mother Goose's Melody* around 1765 and it sometimes has an extra couplet added at the end to make it something of a riddle:

Spell me that in four letters?
I will, THAT.

Or as a pun on selling:

Spell me that without a P
And what a clever scholar you will be.

Pease pudding was a cheap but filling dish made from split yellow peas or lentils and often served with boiled bacon. It is quite smooth and paste-like. The rhyme is sometimes called 'Pease Potage' but I think that would be more like a thick soup.

Children used to sing it to accompany a playground clapping game.

Here Are the Lady's Knives and Forks

Here are the lady's knives and forks,
Here is the lady's table,
Here is the lady's looking glass,
And here is the baby's cradle.

All small children seem to enjoy finger play and although this rhyme was first written down in the nineteenth century, it may well be older. Hands are first held back to back with the fingers interlaced and pointing upwards to show the knives and forks, then, with fingers still interwoven, the hands are turned over to form the table. Next, the two little fingers are held up in a triangle as the mirror and finally the index fingers are raised in a triangle to complete the baby's cradle.

I'm a Little Teapot

I'm a little teapot short and stout,
Here's my handle, here's my spout;
When the tea is made you'll hear me shout,
Tip me up, and pour me out!

I'm a clever teapot,
Yes, it's true,
Here's an example of what I can do,
I can turn my handle into a spout,
Tip me up, and pour me out!

This popular little song of American origin was written by George H. Sanders and Clarence Z. Kelley in 1939. It is usually accompanied by actions to represent the handle, spout and pouring out the tea.

It was written, so the story goes, as a simplified tap dance. Kelley and his wife ran a children's dance school and many of the regular routines were too complex for young children to learn.

Pat-a-Cake, Pat-a-Cake, Baker's Man

Pat-a-cake, pat-a-cake, baker's man,
Bake me a cake as fast as you can;
Pat it and prick it, and mark it with B,
Put it in the oven for baby and me.

'Pat-a-Cake, Pat-a-Cake' was first quoted in 1698, in Thomas Durfey's comic play *The Campaigners*, when the nurse croons it to one of her charges. It next appears in *Mother Goose's Melody* in 1765. The hand-clapping game,

162

often between mother and child, that is still associated with the rhyme perhaps accounts for its longevity as it was passed on through the generations.

Round and Round the Garden

> Round and round the garden,
> Like a teddy bear;
> One step, two step,
> Tickle you under there!

Although they seem such an obvious children's toy now, teddy bears are relatively recent, supposedly named after President Theodore 'Teddy' Roosevelt at the beginning of the twentieth century. This followed a hunting trip in Mississippi in 1902 on which Roosevelt refused to shoot a bear cub, prompting a number of newspaper cartoons and eventually a toy bear named after the president. The rest, as they say, is history.

It's likely the rhyme began shortly after, first recorded in print in the 1940s. As the verse is recited, steps are traced on a child's hand and wrist, ending with them being tickled.

See-Saw, Margery Daw

> See-saw, Margery Daw,
> Jacky shall have a new master;
> He shall have but a penny a day,
> Because he can't work any faster.

Possibly first sung by sawyers to keep rhythm when sawing wood, this has long been chanted by children playing on a see-saw. The rhyme was first printed around 1765 but the earliest references to the game of see-saw date from around 1700, and they are among the oldest amusement rides for children, simply and cheaply put together from spare timber.

The last three lines are sometimes taken to be an allusion to child labour, working for a pittance, particularly in the workhouse. The name Jacky is used here as a generalized boy's name and Margery Daw may just conveniently rhyme with see-saw. The Opies note that Margery was a name for a poor countrywoman in the eighteenth century but it could have other connotations as 'daw' was an archaic term for a 'lazy person', and in Scotland meant 'a slut, slattern or untidy woman'.

This Little Piggy Went to Market

This little piggy went to market,
This little piggy stayed at home,
This little piggy had roast beef,
This little piggy had none,
And this little piggy cried, wee-wee-wee-wee-wee,
I can't find my way home.

This is another very old rhyme. It was first published in
The Famous Tommy Thumb's Little Storybook around 1760
but the first line is quoted in a children's book of 1728. It
is another nursery tickling game where each of the toes are
tweaked in turn, ending with a foot tickle, unless the child
manages to snatch their foot away in time.

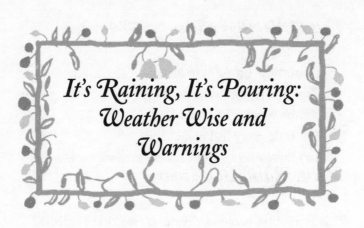

It's Raining, It's Pouring: Weather Wise and Warnings

From early days when cavemen went out hunting and foraging, predicting the weather has always been vitally important. For farmers and sailors, it could be a matter of life and death. A wealth of weather lore developed alongside proverb-type rhymes about the weather and moral warnings. These were passed on through an oral folk tradition for centuries until they were finally written down.

It's Raining, It's Pouring

It's raining, it's pouring,
The old man is snoring;
He went to bed and bumped his head,
And he couldn't get up in the morning.

This first appeared in America in 1939 and although it is widely known, it doesn't have a long history. There have been various attempts to link a specific complaint to the old man's symptoms, mainly to do with brain injuries, but this seems far-fetched.

Rain, Rain, Go Away

> Rain, rain, go away,
> Come again another day.
>
> Rain, rain, go away,
> Come again a Saturday.
>
> Rain, rain, go to Spain,
> Never show your face again.
>
> Rain, rain, go away,
> Come on Martha's wedding day.

In Ancient Greece, it was the custom for children to chant to bring the sun out again, and something very similar to this rhyme would have been known to the Ancient Romans as well as the Greeks. It's possible that children were thought to have a special power to affect the weather.

The rhyme is recorded in a collection of proverbs in 1659, and first appeared with other nursery rhymes at the beginning of the nineteenth century. There are many versions, some linked to festivals or specific days, and there are regional variations. The ones here are just four examples – I wonder what misdemeanour Martha was guilty of to deserve the rain on her wedding day?

The North Wind Doth Blow

The north wind doth blow,
And we shall have snow,
And what will poor robin do then?
Poor thing!
He'll sit in a barn,
To keep himself warm,
And hide his head under his wing.
Poor thing!

Thought to date from Elizabethan times, this nursery rhyme is often best remembered for the evocative illustrations that accompany it, from Arthur Rackham's in the early twentieth century to the more recent ones by Nick Butterworth.

The rhyme was first printed in Britain in *Songs For The Nursery* in 1805, and America in *Mother Goose's Quarto*, around 1825.

For Want of a Nail

> For want of a nail the shoe was lost,
> For want of a shoe the horse was lost,
> For want of a horse the rider was lost,
> For want of a rider the battle was lost,
> For want of a battle the kingdom was lost,
> And all for the want of a horseshoe nail.

As often happens, the first three lines appear to be older than the rest of the verse, dating from a 1640 book by George Herbert called *Outlandish Proverbs*. They could be even older with similarities to a fourteenth-century piece and an old French military proverb, 'The loss of a nail, the loss of an army', recorded in 1629 by the preacher Thomas Adams in one of his sermons.

The Butterfly Effect

The notion of a ripple of increasingly serious consequences from one small incident has resonated through the centuries, with references to the rhyme by the Victorian philanthropist Samuel Smiles, who called it 'the well-known catastrophe', and Benjamin Franklin among others. A framed copy was kept on the wall of the Anglo-American Supply Headquarters in London throughout the Second World War.

My Kingdom for a Horse

There are also enough similarities to Shakespeare's Richard III's cry, 'A horse! A horse! My kingdom for a horse!' for the much cited English king's death at the Battle of Bosworth Field in 1485 to be suggested as the inspiration for the rhyme. He lost his horse when it became stuck in the mud rather than losing a shoe, but an old version of the rhyme using 'knight' in place of 'rider' adds some credibility to the idea as kings were sometimes also called knights.

Mother, May I Go Out to Swim?

> Mother, may I go out to swim?
> Yes, my darling daughter.
> Fold your clothes up neat and trim,
> And don't go near the water.

The rhyme seems to be American in origin, especially as one version includes the line, 'Hang your clothes on a hickory limb'; hickory trees are a native US species, not found in Britain or Europe.

There is some suggestion that this is only part of an older folk song but it does not appear in print until the early twentieth century.

See a Pin and Pick It Up

> See a pin and pick it up,
> All the day you'll have good luck.
> See a pin and let it lay,
> Bad luck you'll have all the day.

Samuel Pepys' diary of 1668 includes a reference to an old English proverb, 'He that will not stoop for a pin will never be worth a pound'. In the Middle Ages, pins were relatively expensive items and husbands would give their wives extra housekeeping money to buy them, which is probably where the term 'pin money' comes from.

Pins were also connected to many superstitions, for instance, a pin left in a bride's dress was considered very unlucky and sailors feared that a pin onboard a ship might result in a leak. At the same time, pins were also thought to guard against witchcraft and were stuck into doorposts or under floorboards for protection.

Halliwell included the verse in his nursery rhyme collection of 1842.

Hush-a-Bye, Baby: Bedtime Lullabies

Lullabies must be one of the oldest forms of song, murmured to babies to rock them to sleep. The gentle rhythms and soothing sounds sometimes disguise less comforting images. There are references to pagan beliefs in nature, magic and good spells, and the occasional hidden royal reference behind many of the best-loved rhymes.

Bye, Baby Bunting

Bye, baby bunting,
Daddy's gone a-hunting,
Gone to get a rabbit skin,
To wrap the baby bunting in.

Bunting is probably a seventeenth-century term of affection meaning plump or chubby, especially when crooned to a baby. The nursery rhyme was first printed in 1784 and there were several other versions where the baby was wrapped in lamb, hare, bull or even lion skin.

Hush-a-Bye, Baby

> Hush-a-bye, baby, on the tree top,
> When the wind blows the cradle will rock;
> When the bough breaks the cradle will fall,
> Down will come baby, cradle, and all.

Also known as 'Rock-a-Bye, Baby', it has been claimed as the first verse to be composed in America. The suggestion is that one of the pilgrims who sailed to the New World on the Mayflower was inspired by Native American mothers hanging birch-bark cradles from trees for the wind to rock their babies.

French Fables and Saxon Boughs

However, it may predate the Pilgrim Fathers. Joseph Ritson, an eighteenth-century contemporary of Samuel Johnson, was an avid collector of old songs and ballads, and he believed the rhyme originated from a French fable in which a nurse warns about a baby falling while a wolf waits below. Others have identified 'bye' as an old English word for sleep and suggest the first line ended with 'on the green boh' – 'boh' being a Saxon word for bough which would have been pronounced 'bock', rhyming with 'rock'.

A Papist Plot?

The rhyme is sung to a version of 'Lilliburlero', the tune of which is also used for 'There Was an Old Woman Tossed Up in a Basket', and like that nursery rhyme it has been linked to the Stuart kings, in this case James II. In 1688, there was a widespread rumour that James's son and heir from his second marriage was not really his baby but a substitute smuggled into the nursery in a warming pan; never mind the unfeasibility of this, it was all part of a papist plot to ensure a future Catholic monarch on the British throne. So the cradle stood for the Stuarts, and the wind could be seen as the Protestant wind that would save England, ushering in the Glorious Revolution and Protestant King William and Queen Mary.

Pride Comes Before a Fall

We do know for certain that it was first published in *Mother Goose's Melody* around 1765 where it appeared with a curious footnote: 'This may serve as a Warning to the Proud and Ambitious, who climb so high that they generally fall at last.' This may mean that at the time, a deeper satirical meaning was understood to lie behind the verse.

Rock-a-Bye, Baby

Rock-a-bye, baby,
Thy cradle is green,
Father's a nobleman,
Mother's a queen,
And Betty's a lady,
And wears a gold ring,
And Johnny's a drummer,
And drums for the king.

This was a popular alternative version of 'Hush-a-Bye, Baby', which appeared in *Songs For The Nursery* at the beginning of the nineteenth century.

I See the Moon

I see the moon, and the moon sees me,
God bless the moon, and God bless me.

For fishermen:

I see the moon and the moon sees me,
God bless the sailors on the sea.

Also:

> I see the moon and the moon sees me,
> The moon sees the somebody I'd like to see;
> God bless the moon and God bless me,
> God bless the somebody I'd like to see.

The last was seen as a blessing or 'good' spell to ward away evil and draw someone to you. All of these couplets link pagan beliefs about the moon and magic with the Christian God, and may have a long folk history.

There were many superstitions connected to the moon. New moons in particular were seen as lucky, and children used to bow when they saw one. Turning over the coins in your pocket when the new moon first rose was said to bring good luck.

Matthew, Mark, Luke, and John

Matthew, Mark, Luke, and John,
Bless the bed that I lie on.
Four corners to my bed,
Four angels round my head;
One to watch and one to pray,
And two to bear my soul away.

This nursery rhyme or prayer is also known as the 'White Paternoster'. It has echoes of an ancient Babylonian prayer and a medieval Jewish prayer with the idea of angels behind, before and at both sides. The earliest Christian version seems to date from Germany in the late Middle Ages, although Chaucer refers to a 'White Paternoster' in *The Miller's Tale* around 1387, which could be the same prayer.

Otherwise, its first appearance in English is in a book called *A Candle In The Dark, Or, A Treatise Concerning The Nature Of Witches And Witchcraft*, by Thomas Ady. Writing in 1656, Ady told the story of an old woman from Essex who blessed herself with many 'Popish Charms' including this one.

The prayer became so popular that during the nineteenth century, visiting clergy complained that in some areas children knew this 'night-spell' better than 'The Lord's Prayer'.

Star Light, Star Bright

> Star light, star bright,
> The first star I see tonight;
> I wish I may, I wish I might,
> Have the wish I wish tonight.

There is always something exciting and magical about glimpsing a shooting star, and it's easy to see how the superstition of wishing on one as it falls might have started in the ancient world. The idea of wishing on the first star

of the evening is more recent, and this rhyme first appeared in America in the late nineteenth century.

It soon spread to Britain and has since become known worldwide through Disney and other film references.

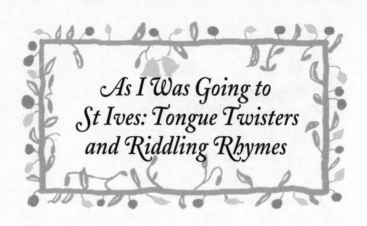

As I Was Going to St Ives: Tongue Twisters and Riddling Rhymes

Many well-known tongue twisters have their roots in ancient sayings, passed on orally, and written down only relatively recently. They are essentially rhymes that rely heavily on alliteration, making them very difficult to say, which is reflected in their apt American title, 'word cramps'.

The concentration needed to recite them correctly means they have been used since the Middle Ages to help with a range of speech impediments, including lisping. For this reason they remain popular with public speakers, actors and broadcasters to practise before a performance.

Like tongue twisters, riddling rhymes have been popular for centuries. Examples have even been found in Ancient Greek and Latin texts. Many popular nursery rhymes, including 'Humpty Dumpty', have their origins in riddles.

Around the Rugged Rocks

> Robert Rutter dreamed a dream,
> He dreamt he saw a raging bear,
> Rush from the rugged rocks,
> And around the rugged rocks
> The ragged rascal ran.

The familiar tongue twister, 'Around the rugged rocks the ragged rascal ran', was once part of this longer verse, which may be medieval in origin.

Three Grey Geese

> Three grey geese in the green grass grazing,
> Grey were the geese, and green was the grazing.

This is another, very old tongue twister, its roots lost in folklore. Jean Harrowven, writing in *Origins Of Rhymes, Songs And Sayings*, suggests it may be among the oldest still known.

Three Crooked Cripples

Three crooked cripples went through Cripplegate.
And through Cripplegate went three crooked cripples.
Hickup, snickup, rise up, right up.
Three drops in the cup are good for the hiccups.

My grandmother insisted that reciting 'Peter Piper' without taking a breath would cure hiccups. I'm afraid I was never convinced but apparently she was not alone in this idea; tongue twisters were widely thought to help, as shown in the words of 'Three Crooked Cripples'.

Perhaps for the cure to work you need to follow the advice of the nineteenth-century satirist, Hewson Clarke, who was best known for libelling Lord Byron. Clarke suggested repeating 'Peter Piper' – '… in my younger days a particular favourite with me … three times without drawing breath' – this he felt 'renders it a useful lesson in the art of elocution'. I have to say I'm not sure it's possible.

Peter Piper Picked a Peck

Peter Piper picked a peck of pickled pepper;
A peck of pickled pepper Peter Piper picked;
If Peter Piper picked a peck of pickled pepper,
Where's the peck of pickled pepper Peter Piper picked?

Peter Piper was first printed in *Peter Piper's Practical Principles of Plain and Perfect Pronunciation* (the title itself something of a tongue tripper) by John Harris in London, in 1813. The book included a tongue twister for each letter of the alphabet. However, the rhyme seems to have been well known long before this date.

There is speculation that Peter Piper was based on a real person, an eighteenth-century administrator for the French East India Company called Pierre Poivre. He introduced spices, including pepper, to Mauritius from the Americas, and investigated the potential of the Seychelles for the lucrative spice trade.

As I Was Going to St Ives

> As I was going to St Ives,
> I met a man with seven wives,
> Each wife had seven sacks,
> Each sack had seven cats,
> Each cat had seven kits:
> Kits, cats, sacks and wives,
> How many were there going to St Ives?

The answer is one or none depending on how you read the question. It's generally assumed that the rhyme refers to St Ives in Cornwall, although St Ives in Cambridgeshire is another contender.

This riddle was first printed around 1730, although that version had nine wives each with nine sacks. But this particular form of riddle within a rhyme is very old. In fact, something astonishingly similar was found in the 'Rhind Mathematical Papyrus' dating from between 1600 and 1800 BC. It even has seven houses and seven cats, although this was most likely meant as an arithmetical problem rather than a riddle. The Opies also found a Latin version from around 1200 with seven men travelling to Rome, with seven donkeys, seven sacks and so on.

As Soft As Silk

As soft as silk,
As white as milk,
As bitter as gall;
A thick wall,
And a green coat covers me all.

What am I? A walnut.

This riddle appeared in the *Booke Of Meery Riddles* in 1600 and has been reproduced regularly in English ever since. Similar rhymes can be found in German and French.

In Marble Walls As White As Milk

In marble walls as white as milk,
Lined with a skin as soft as silk,
Within a fountain crystal-clear,
A golden apple doth appear.
No doors there are to this stronghold,
Yet thieves break in and steal the gold.

What is being described? An egg.

This made its first appearance in chapbooks towards the end of the eighteenth century, then a few years later in a manuscript collection of riddles, jokes and charades. Eggs were a popular subject for riddles and it is thought that 'Humpty Dumpty' was originally intended as one.

Little Nancy Etticoat

Little Nancy Etticoat,
With a white petticoat,
And a red nose;
She has no feet or hands,
The longer she stands
The shorter she grows.

Confused? The answer is a candle.

Riddle rhymes have had a lasting appeal and this one goes back to the mid-seventeenth century, although other names are sometimes given including Nanny Goat and Miss Hetty Cote. 'Lütt Johann Öölken' in German is effectively the same rhyme.

Two Legs Sat Upon Three Legs

Two legs sat upon three legs,
With one leg in his lap;
In comes four legs
And runs away with one leg;
Up jumps two legs,
Catches up three legs,
Throws it after four legs,
And makes him bring back one leg.

This also appeared in the *Booke Of Meery Riddles* of 1600 with versions in German, and can possibly trace its origins back to the Venerable Bede's writings. It has a more convoluted solution, which lends itself to a fun sequence of illustrations, perhaps the reason it has stayed so popular and been included in so many nursery-rhyme collections.

The story is that a man sits on a three-legged stool with a leg of mutton in his lap. A dog walks in and steals the mutton leg. The man jumps up, grabs the stool and throws it at the dog, forcing him to return the joint of meat.

Bibliography

Carpenter, H., and Pritchard, M., *The Oxford Companion To Children's Literature* (Oxford University Press, 1984)

Folklore, Myths And Legends Of Britain (Reader's Digest, 1973)

Fraser, Antonia, *Mary Queen Of Scots* (Weidenfeld & Nicolson, 1994)

Gash, Norman, *Aristocracy And People: Britain 1815–1865* (Arnold, 1979)

Halliwell, James Orchard, *The Nursery Rhymes Of England* (The Bodley Head, 1970)

Harrowven, Jean, *Origins Of Rhymes, Songs And Sayings* (Pryor Publications, 1998)

Latham, Robert, *The Shorter Pepys* (Bell & Hyman, 1985)

Loades, D. M., *Politics And The Nation 1450–1660* (Harvester Press/Fontana, 1974)

Mortimer, Ian, *The Time Traveller's Guide To Elizabethan England* (The Bodley Head, 2012)

Opie, Iona and Peter (eds), *The Oxford Dictionary Of Nursery Rhymes* (Oxford University Press, 1951 and 1971)

Opie, Iona and Peter (eds), *The Oxford Nursery Rhyme Book* (Oxford University Press, 1955)

Palmer, A. W., *A Dictionary Of Modern History* (Penguin, 1985)

Picard, Liza, *Dr. Johnson's London* (Weidenfeld & Nicolson, 2000)

Seward, Desmond, *Richard III: England's Black Legend* (Watts, 1984)

Untermeyer, Louis, *The Golden Treasury Of Poetry* (Collins, 1969)

www.rhymes.org.uk

www.mamalisa.com

www.oed.com

The eighteenth- and nineteenth-century anthologies referred to most often are:

Tommy Thumb's Pretty Song Book (1744)

Mother Goose's Melody; Or Sonnets For The Cradle (1765), registered as a published book by T. Carnan (1780)

Gammer Gurton's Garland (1784)

Infant Institutes (1797)

Christmas Box (1797)

The Newest Christmas Box (1797)

Mother Goose's Quarto: Or Melodies Complete (Munroe and Francis, Boston, Massachusetts, 1825)

James Orchard Halliwell, *The Nursery Rhymes Of England*, first printed 1842.

Index of First Lines